addicted

addicted

NOTES FROM THE BELLY OF THE BEAST
edited by Lorna Crozier & Patrick Lane

GREYSTONE BOOKS
DOUGLAS & McINTYRE
PUBLISHING GROUP
VANCOUVER/TORONTO

With special thanks to the press's editor, the remarkable Barbara Pulling.
—L.C. and P.L.

Greystone Books
A division of Douglas & McIntyre Ltd.
2323 Quebec Street, Suite 201
Vancouver, British Columbia V5T 4S7
www.greystonebooks.com

National Library of Canada Cataloguing in Publication Data

Main entry under title:
Addicted

ISBN 1-55054-886-7

1. Addicts—Psychology. 2. Dependency (Psychology) 3. Authors,
Canadian (English)—20th century—Biography.* I. Crozier, Lorna, 1948–
II. Lane, Patrick, 1939–
BF575.D34A32 2001   155.2'32   C2001-910877-X

Editing by Barbara Pulling
Copy-editing by Naomi Pauls
Text design and typesetting by Julie Cochrane
Cover design and photography by Jacqueline Verkley
Printed and bound in Canada by Friesens
Printed on acid-free paper

We gratefully acknowledge the financial support of the Canada Council for
the Arts, the British Columbia Ministry of Tourism, Small Business and
Culture, and the Government of Canada through the Book Publishing
Industry Development Program (BPIDP) for our publishing activities.

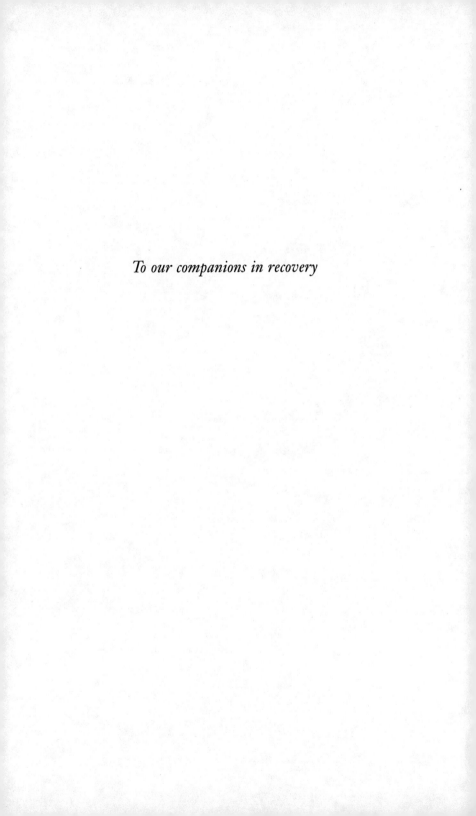

To our companions in recovery

Contents

Preface / xi

Preface

Over the past twenty-five years, I've sat in many a smoky kitchen with friends, all of us telling stories of parties, conferences, festivals and other events where we'd gathered as writers. There was always a bottle of wine in the middle of the table, a case of beer in the fridge, and a twenty-six of whisky on the counter next to the sink. Funny and outrageous, our stories circled around booze and drugs, though the words *alcoholism* and *addiction* were never mentioned.

I don't regret the experiences we shared, but things are different now. The bottles may still be on kitchen tables and counters somewhere, but where I've been sitting for some time now, the spectre of addiction has added a cautionary note to our behaviour and our tales.

Some of this country's most revered and influential writers—Margaret Laurence, Alden Nowlan, Gwendolyn

MacEwen, John Thompson, Marian Engel, Al Purdy, to name a few—were close companions of the bottle. Sometimes you catch glimpses of this affinity in their fiction or poetry, but none of them left us with an autobiographical account. As I pondered the role alcohol has played in my own life, I couldn't help but wonder what these glorious writers would have said about the topic and what a difference their words might have made to those who read them. Out of such ruminations came the idea for this book.

The first name of my own generation that came to mind was David Adams Richards. David is not only a gifted writer but also a great raconteur. Some of the stories I've heard him tell in his rich New Brunswick lilt have been about his drinking days. Full of humour, self-deprecation and an incredible, charming honesty, they hold listeners enthralled. If he agreed to put his words on paper, I thought, I'd take it as a sign to approach others. I hesitated to phone him. Talking around the table and writing things down for the whole world to see are very different propositions. But David's response to my request was an immediate "Great idea." He said that though he'd written about alcoholism in his novels, he'd never done so in a more personal account, and it was "about time" he did.

David's "about time" confirmed my sense that this was the right moment for such a book. After he accepted, I asked Patrick Lane to share the task of editing. He and I have been together for more than two decades, and for the last while we'd been living with his struggles to get sober. Our mutual breaking of the silence around alcoholism became an act of faith. If we were going to ask others to write about their addictions, we needed to do it ourselves.

There are more than two hundred types of twelve-step groups in North America. Though the addictions they address vary from alcohol to food to emotional crises, all emphasize the necessity of anonymity. When you walk into that church basement or community centre, you are guaranteed that what you say and who you are will remain behind closed doors. The writers who accepted our invitation to compose an original piece for *Addicted* broke this first rule. They stepped out, gave their full names, and put their lives on the line. I can't emphasize enough the courage of this act.

Those who know little about substance abuse see it as something unsavoury and shameful. Why don't the drunks, the junkies, the smokers, the bulimics just smarten up? Pull themselves up by the bootstraps. Get some willpower. Stop. There's also a touch of the romantic about the wild, self-destructive painter or poet who shatters complacency and taboos. Counteracting these simplistic attitudes toward addiction, the writers in this collection give us the bare bones of their reality. Many said that writing about this part of their lives gave them new insights into where they had been and what they had become. That was an advantage none of us had predicted. Most had agreed to take the risk in the hope that their stories would help someone else.

The books that readers cherish make them feel less alone.

No one is lonelier than addicts and those who are part of their lives. Six of the writers here share an addiction to alcohol; in our culture that remains the common drug of choice. It is, after all, legal and easy to get. One writer talks about smoking, another heroin, and another an obsession with food and pharmaceuticals. But whatever their demons, these writers offer a view of a world rarely seen in our literature. Because they were brave enough to speak openly about their experiences, without self-pity or false justifications, their essays break through the isolation and loneliness that addiction creates. Each is a gift, offering the possibility of healing and hope.

—Lorna Crozier

Counting
the Bones

Patrick Lane

I start on my knees. It's the position of prayer, but an alcoholic neither knows nor understands prayer. I am naked and my knees press into the clean white tiles. My forearms rest on the rim of a mottled white bowl. It is six o'clock in the morning in a hotel somewhere in Toronto. I don't remember the name of the hotel. It's just a hotel, a place of anonymous safety, a continent away from where I live. My hands grip the toilet bowl as I dry-heave yet again, there being nothing in my stomach to throw up except for a few glaucous strings of phlegm. They hang from my lips until they fall into the bowl in turgid knots. I stare into a sea where nothing lives. My abdomen tightens into a fist and punches at my stomach as it tries to force out what is no longer there, the alcohol of the long, pitiful night.

I heave again and again, unable to stop this belly cramp.

I'm crying, but I'm not aware of that, not yet. Tears and sweat are much the same after you've drunk thirty ounces of alcohol and snorted two grams of cocaine. Three more surges and the first blood comes, a few drops that splash into the snot-skewed water. They drop and flower there like the lost blossoms of a geranium, a heavy red, bright with oxygen. They are like the blossoms that grow on the fists of a man who strikes a cement wall so he can feel something, anything, himself. It is blood from an artery. I see this and wonder at it as I heave again. There is in my mind a kind of grim amusement at this flowering. I would laugh if I could. The next spasm brings more, a tablespoon of blood that drowns the delicate flowers that shimmered there a moment before. I am somehow sorry to see them go. Another, and my mouth fills with blood. It boils across my tongue, through my lips and into the bowl.

My body shakes and trembles with a terrible palsy. I am covered with thin sweat. My feet and hands are cold. It is as if my heart can't find the way to fuel those parts of me that shine out into touching. There is no feeling in them. They hang from my limbs like the heavy books my teachers used to make me hold at arm's length to punish me. When my arms could no longer hold the books out straight, I was strapped for weakness.

When was that?

Too long ago.

I get up carefully, wipe my face with a stained washcloth,

and stumble to the bed. I sit down heavily, stare past my belly at my flaccid sex, my thighs and feet. They belong to someone else. I balance precariously. I can't lie down. Not yet. I take a cigarette from the packet on the bedside table, light it, and pull blue smoke into my lungs. I feel the dizziness as my arteries contract, and I almost faint. I am rocking slowly but I'm unaware of that, just as I'm unaware of my tears. It is a rocking in time with my beating heart.

I look back at the bedside table and reach for the bottle of vodka. I unscrew the white plastic cap, lift the bottle to my lips, and take a small drink, anything to stop the shakes and nausea. I have already forgotten about the blood. It's as if the vomiting occurred somewhere in the deep past, so long ago it is barely remembered by the animal I am. The alcohol slides past my acid-burned throat and hits my stomach like a rock striking thin water. The liquor sits there for a brief moment and then I'm back on my knees by the toilet bowl, puking again. There is only a little blood this time. I feel relieved and yet somehow disappointed. Surely there is more blood in me than that? What's wrong with my body that it will not obey?

Back to the bed, where I lift the cigarette from the ashtray, almost burned down to the filter, take a drag, and then pick up the bottle again, swallowing two or three ounces. I know I have to get the alcohol past my stomach and into my intestines, where it can be absorbed by my bloodstream. Only then will I feel better. It works. This time my stomach holds on, and in a minute or two I feel the drowsy steadiness in my muscles and brain. My body slows and the nausea begins to disappear. I take another drink and then another, until I have six or seven ounces in me. Only then do I lie down, light another cigarette from the last one, and stare over my feet at the city as it begins its terrible anonymous day. The traffic noise is a vague and persistent buzz.

There is no more cocaine. I check the wrappers, but they have been licked clean sometime in the night. My nose is bleeding now, the small sores cracked open by my puking. In four hours I have an interview on national radio and in six hours with a national newspaper. I have a reading at eight o'clock tonight in a bar somewhere off Yonge Street. I close my eyes, not to sleep, but to lie in the dark of my body.

The heavy drinking has begun again, but it's never really stopped. I've been dry-drunk a few weeks here and there in the past three years. Dry-drunk. An alcoholic waiting until he can drink again. I think of the word *wrath*, the word *punishment*, the word . . . what word? Why not joy, contentment, serenity, peace?

⌒

Two months later, I sit in my office and try to remember when my addiction started. That's what it is: an addiction, a disease. I try to remember my first drink, but it's too far away, lost in clouds and rain. Perhaps it was in my mother's womb, or passed to me in my mother's milk. It could have been the sips of beer my mother or father gave me as a child when they were drinking. I loved the taste of beer, the froth, the bubbles, so different from orange pop or Coca-Cola. I know I was thirteen when I had my first serious drink. My parents had left me home to baby-sit on New Year's Eve. While my sister and brother slept, I opened the liquor cupboard beside the fridge. Inside were vodka, rye whisky, dark Navy rum and lemon gin.

I got a tumbler from beside the sink and poured some of each bottle into the glass until it was full. I drank the liquor quickly out of fear I would be caught. I was instantly, totally drunk, and I loved the feeling. Within ten minutes I was in the back yard, throwing up in the garden. When I finished puking I went back into the kitchen, poured another glass full of the mix of liquors, and drank it. This time I didn't vomit. How much did I keep down? Probably five or six ounces. Thinking of it now, I wonder I didn't kill myself. Instead, I simply stumbled upstairs to bed and passed out.

Did I inherit this madness? Was it in my father's seed or my mother's egg? What history I know of my family on both sides is terrible, full of the dead and the dying, the raging, the infirm, a man, my grandfather, drunk, burying my father's mother, my grandmother, under a caragana hedge so she would be of use and fertilize the earth on the farm near Pincher Creek, Alberta. Why let her body go to waste in a graveyard? Or so my grandfather thought. My father ran away from home shortly afterwards. He was thirteen. There are too many stories, too much for me to remember. I sat drunk with my mother when she was drunker, two years after my father was murdered, her telling me of their life together, stories I should never have heard, her raising her skirt to her pudenda and saying, Daddy always called me Hairless Joe. I didn't know if it was my father or her father she spoke of, mumbling from her chair, her white thighs glaring in the lamplight, her shaking hands gripping her whisky, my sorrow.

As a teenager I was full of pretension about literary things. I thought William Blake's line from his *Proverbs*, "The road of excess leads to the palace of wisdom," meant that, in order to achieve wisdom, you must live with complete abandon. Sex, drugs, the wild dance; a lack of tolerance, wisdom, grace. I had confused Blake with Rimbaud. But it didn't matter. Nothing did.

Strange how you remember things: Saturday night in the mid-fifties, with a case of beer bought from the Capitol Taxi bootlegger. I drank it all in a few hours with friends and then drove off alone in search of a girl, any girl, a dirt road, a car parked under slow lonesome trees and tearing off my clothes as she tore hers off and making, what? Love, perhaps, or what I thought love was back then, drunken, crazy sex without any responsibility for her or for myself. Elvis Presley had just reinvented the world. Rock 'n' roll, the postwar bounty years awash with money, my father with a new car, a house he owned, me striding through school with Ezra Pound and Eliot on my mind, arrogant and confused. I drank every weekend and sometimes during the week if I could get a half-case of beer or a mickey. Sometimes I shared the liquor, but most times I drank it alone.

The daily drinking began in my early twenties. I was married with three kids by then and there wasn't much money for liquor, but when there was the smallest amount left over it went for cheap wine or a bottle of port that I sipped at to make last as long as possible, a night or two at most, while I sat up late struggling with my wretched early poems. The sixties almost finished me. It was a decade of death and loss starting with my brother's little girl, five years old, dying of cancer. That was 1962. In 1964, my brother, older than I by three years, died in Vancouver of a brain hemorrhage. He was a poet as well, one of the wild Lane boys of myth and legend. My family reeled at the deaths. I think I went mad then, but so did we all, two other brothers, a sister, my mother. Four years later my father was gunned down at his office by a drunken customer with a grudge. My mother-in-law had died only a few weeks earlier.

Three months after my father's death I got up from the kitchen table and walked out the door, leaving my wife and children behind. I had eight dollars in my pocket and the shirt on my back. I have only fragments of memory from that time: a huge rainstorm east of Calgary and me lying in a ditch, drenched and shaking; the dusty roads of Saskatchewan; the cars and trucks that picked me up and took me across the country. On the University of Toronto campus I bought a collection of Garcia Lorca's poems with my last, sad dollar. I read it on the lawn surrounded by students walking to their classes.

I stayed in Toronto through the spring and summer, living on the street, drinking what I begged or stole in the bars on Spadina and Queen, until I hitchhiked west and re-appeared at my front door in Vancouver. My marriage lasted four more months. We split up, my wife remarried, and I was gone. I had a beater of a car, a thousand dollars I'd borrowed from my mother, a fifty-pound Remington typewriter in the trunk with a sheaf of canary-yellow paper, and a couple of bottles of whisky on the seat beside me. I was headed directly for self-destruction.

The next few years I wandered the continent in a blur of casual affairs, casual friendships, communards and hippies, criminals and crazies. I lived in a series of crippled Volks-wagen vans in various stages of repair, or in the apartment of whichever girl was willing to put up with me for a week or two while I ate her food and enjoyed her body. I slept in alleys, in cardboard boxes, on rooftops, surviving through the usual petty crimes and misdemeanours. I belonged nowhere. I was utterly alone and I wanted it that way: just me, a bottle, a bag of drugs. That I wrote book after book of poems during this time leaves me bewildered now. I was completely addicted to alcohol by then. The drugs I could take or leave: opium, hashish, grass, cocaine, acid, amphetamines. They were deco-rations on the Christmas tree bottle that was always with me.

Where does all this leave me now, in my sixty-first year? Still addicted, moving from abstinence to excess and back to abstinence at a rate that would stagger most people or kill them, ranging through shame, guilt, self-pity, anger, despair, doubt and confusion.

I have a disease. Ten years ago I would have laughed at such a notion. Booze and drugs and tobacco are available everywhere, and I choose to use them. But what do I do when they start using me? What do I do when I'm on my knees puking blood, only to go right back to the bottle? The straight and sane people of this ordinary world have little time for drunks and users. Addicts and alcoholics steal and lie and cheat. Sometimes they maim or kill. They can't be trusted by anyone, least of all themselves. Their souls are drowned in a bottle or rolled up in a five-dollar bill. They travel through remorse until it sticks like a bone in their throats. They ask for forgiveness only to betray it ten minutes later in a bar with a second double chilling in a shaky hand.

I've been there. I know that place.

A lot of my friends are addicts and alcoholics, people who live in excess, their bodies driven by what owns them. Given the moment, given the particular day or night, given the desperation, most of them would sell their mothers for a bottle, an eight-ball, a paper or two of heroin and a needle. Some are in jail or in rehab centres. Some are dead. The writers and artists of this country who've wasted their talents and their lives are legion. Gwendolyn MacEwen, Milton Acorn, but so many others. Johnny hanging from an electrical cord in the Blackstone Hotel on Granville Street; Jimmy dead with a needle still in his arm two weeks out of rehab, overestimating his tolerance, his body wrapped around a toilet in China-town; Debra selling herself to anyone for another trip to the shooting gallery, her eyes filled with pitiful, sordid despair, until she was found in a dumpster in Montreal.

I know where they've been because I've been there. The spectres, the ghosts live with me. I only have to go back and remember and the madness returns. I see myself driving down the frozen midnight highway somewhere in British Columbia with one eye closed, because the road ahead veers off wildly in two directions. I drive like that for three hundred miles, my eyelid practised at the manoeuvre, then suddenly find myself in a field fifty miles west of Prince George with barbed wire wrapped across my spidered windshield like coiled rib-bons, my head bleeding from hitting the wheel.

Or is it two years later, my car rolling on the 401, the third accident in four months? In each accident I've lost con-sciousness. This time my car catches the gravel as I pass a semi. The tires crack to the side and the car heels over and up and I say to myself, This time I want to stay awake and see what it's like, full of drunken bravado. But after the third roll I'm unconscious again. I awake to a guy speaking quietly to me through the side window of the upside-down car: "Jesus, you okay? You rolled eight times." I'm angry. I saw only three rolls before I was out. Whisky and wine drip from the ceiling, there's glass everywhere. The Ontario police escort me to a little local hospital and then let me go, why, I'll never know. My Quebec licence plates, maybe. The hospital kicks me out with a broken collarbone. Bits of glass glaze my cheeks and hands. Go back to your own province, they say. Get treated there. I stagger out into the night and through the streets of some lost little nowhere town, find the highway west, and start walking, the wind hard off Lake Ontario. In ten hours I'm in Toronto, drinking in a cheap hotel room with a girl who's struggling with my belt and zipper while I take just one more drink from her bottle. She's some hippie girl from England, stoned herself, the Summer of Love just a few short years behind both of us.

I sit here in the night and I count my shattered bones. It's as good a way as any to chart my life. Everything seems to begin with the broken. Two toes, but I was only a boy, so they don't count. A shattered ankle, the doctor happy, he tells me, because he only gets two or three breaks this bad in a lifetime. Your ankle's cornflakes, he says, and puts it together with fifteen pins. A stoned, drunken jump off a thirty-foot cliff into shallow water at my mother's seventy-fifth birthday reunion. Right leg broken, hit by a car outside a bar. A clean break, though, with friendly nurses. Four lumbar vertebrae, same cliff jump, except the doctors didn't notice the compression fractures then. Three cervical vertebrae, discovered ten years later by my chiropractor. I'm shorter now by an inch or two. Third finger, left hand, setting chokers up on Sugar Lake, hungover and tired. Both forearms, multiple fractures, not drunk, simply foolish as a boy in high school. Collarbone from the Highway 401 crash, left shoulder distorted one inch. Shoulder blade, slipping as I stumbled drunk downstairs. Broken nose in a barroom fight, one punch by a kid not as drunk as me and then down on the floor looking for my glasses. Concussion from falling out a window onto my head. Scars? Too many to count. Injuries that should've killed me but didn't through some crazed good luck. God protects the drunk and the stupid.

But that's only my body. What else have I broken? Families, wives, children, lovers, friends, brothers, sister, mother, father. They wander out there. Or maybe they don't, and I am locked again in self-pity and ego, thinking I have changed the world by my actions, my endless preoccupation with myself. And is all this confession excessive? Am I healing here?

The past is a burden I carry on my shoulder. On the other shoulder is the future. Right here is this one moment, twisting perfectly as it must in the is-ness of now. And now what? Go back and find the dead, to murmur my loss in whispers of dust? Take into my arms my niece, my brother, my father and wish them alive again; gather my children, my grandchildren, my friends and tell them I am sorry? Kneel at my woman's feet and beg forgiveness? Sorrow is a root that grows from the heart, and the heart has no cure but love. I suffer, but who does not?

I am confused and sometimes dismayed at what the world

is, now I am recovering. Ice and snow, vodka and cocaine. Stand on a street corner in any city and watch for a moment as drugs change hands, a hooker working her life away to pay for her pimp's habit and her own. Look for the men who stand in the shadows as they wait for the liquor store to open, hiding ten steps away from the sound of a door unlocking. After you've done that, go to a place where you can walk into a room, sit down, and, when it comes your turn, say, Hello, I'm Patrick. I'm an alcoholic. Start by telling your story to others, the ones who know where you have been, as you pray for the years before and behind you, the year you're living now, the night, the day, this hour, this minute, this one.

My Father, Myself

Marnie Woodrow

L ooking back, I can see that I had several fathers. Some of them were easier to love than others. I've been different people at different times in my life, too. And some of them were easier to *be* than others. My father drank too much and, for a time, so did I. Something made him continue to drink; something made me pause halfway along the path.

There's a man in a black snowsuit and a red toque: I call him Daddy. His cheeks are chubby, pink from the cold. He tows me up and down a snow-covered hill, pulling the toboggan with big strong arms. He gives in to me whenever I beg, "One more time, plee-ease!" and then carries me all the way home on his shoulders. I spend Saturday afternoons watching him fix cars as he laughs with his friends. He has a lot of friends in our small town. I decide he's famous because he owns a garage.

I'm in charge of sweeping the floors of the garage with a big push broom. Left alone with a seemingly endless supply of pale-blue paper, I draw pictures in a room that smells of motor oil and axle grease. I write my name over and over and make up stories. I know the words *carburetor, alternator, starter* and *alignment*, although I can't yet write them down. If I'm good, my daddy takes me across the street to his friend's garage, where they have a rack that lifts cars right off the ground. I ride up and down on the rack, knowing my mother would be furious if she saw me doing this. Then one day my daddy's garage isn't a place we go to any more. My mother tells me it belongs to someone else now. Oh. When we drive past it I feel sad. I hate the people who took it away from my daddy. He seems to hate them too.

I'm a little older: he's Dad now. He teaches me to throw and catch a baseball; he teaches me to bait a hook without crying. Sometimes I think he forgets that I'm a girl; I go into the house wailing because he hits me with a puck while we're playing hockey on the rink he made for me in our yard. My voice is accusatory as I tell my mother, "Dad tried to kill me!" But I still know that this is the man who buys me chips and gum just because I ask. He watches baseball games on a black-and-white TV that he carries outside and plugs into the exterior wall of the house. While the announcer shouts out "Home Run!" and "Bases Loaded!", my dad fixes our car even if it isn't broken. He stays out there in the dark, by the light of the flickering television, a cooler of beer at his feet.

He works for someone else now, selling car parts from behind a counter. He's not happy when he comes to the dinner table carrying a bottle of beer. I tell him at least now he can keep his fingernails clean, but he doesn't smile. The bottle of beer is always beside him, cold and salty. Sometimes he lets me have a sip.

Our house is situated at the bottom of a hill where two streets merge. My dad sits on a lawn chair on the front porch, sipping beer and frowning. Cars come racing down the hill and sometimes they don't quite stop at the stop sign. My dad runs into the street shouting "Hey!" and "Stop!!!", waving his fist. His anger lasts for hours. He keeps a pen handy to write down the licence plate numbers of the offending cars. I try not to be in the yard when he does these things. He's usually a soft-spoken man, but when he yells my stomach turns to ice water. I've never heard anyone sound so angry before. I pray that he will never yell at me like that. I decide he's angry because he doesn't have a job. He "lost" it. I now know that he lost the garage, too. A lot of things seem to be going missing these days. My mother promises me that everything is fine; she tells me that my dad is angry about the cars that don't quite stop because he's worried one of the kids in the neighbourhood will be killed by *one of those jerks*. Oh.

The man I call Dad smells like mouthwash, stale sweat and onions. His shirt isn't tucked in, his nose is red like Rudolph's. He tells me to wait in the car because he has to "pick something up." I wait and wait. It's getting dark outside and I'm bored. I stare at the bottle of Scope on the floor of the car. Apparently my dad is very worried about having bad breath. I read advertising flyers out loud in the dim light and hunt for candies and gum, singing to myself. For a man without a job he seems to have a lot of errands. When we pull out of the parking lot he drives so slowly I want to scream. I don't realize that he's worse than the people who don't stop at the stop sign in front of our house, that he's drunk as he drives me all over town. All I know is that he doesn't laugh or smile very much, and if I whine he gets mad and tells me I'm a baby.

When we get home my mother looks at him as if she doesn't like him any more. Sometimes I think she's being mean to him; other times I can see that she's been crying. "Where the hell were you?" she hisses in a cracked voice. When she kisses me and tucks me in, she asks me where I went with Dad. I usually say "We went to Peter's House." Peter's House is synonymous with driving home on the wrong side of the road. I hear the words *I can't take much more, Bill* echoing through the house late at night. I lie awake listening for the sound of my mother packing a suitcase and leaving me behind. She doesn't, but I never stop worrying about it.

My dad loves me. My mother tells me this over and over. He's having a hard time right now, that's all. She buys him a beautiful blue suit and a leather briefcase. He looks fat and handsome in his suit, but I don't know why he needs a briefcase. He doesn't seem to like working; if he gets a job, he loses it. I'm not supposed to think that my dad's bad moods have anything to do with me. I'm a good girl; he loves me and everything is going to be fine. But I'm worried we're going to have to move to the Poor House. My mother takes me with her whenever she goes to visit friends. Her friends don't come to our house because it's a pigsty. I learn the word *ashamed*, which is much easier to spell than carburetor. My dad isn't always very nice. He calls my friend Charles a *bloody pansy*. Charles hears him, and I never bring a friend home with me again.

When I go downstairs to watch cartoons my dad is there, asleep on the sofa. He's cranky if I wake him up, so I try not to. The only time he doesn't sleep on the downstairs sofa is when my grandpa comes to visit. Before Grandpa arrives my mom and I clean the house for hours. My dad is very messy, and my mother likes things to be tidy. I think this must be why they fight so much. I keep my room neat and try to stay in it for as long as possible. The rest of the house doesn't feel good. I draw and write a lot, because every other game seems too noisy against the silence. My parents get along better when my grandpa's around. I wish he would come and live with us so my mother would be happy like that every day. She loves her daddy. I wish I could love mine without trying.

We go to church on Sundays because God is going to help my father drink less beer. The basement fridge is full of big bottles of Pepsi and 7-Up. My dad has a bookmark that says "God grant me the serenity to accept the things I cannot change, the courage to change the things I can, and the wisdom to know the difference." I don't know what it means, but I like the sound of it. My dad has a psychiatrist. He goes to AA meetings and something called *therapy*. I go to meetings too. At them I meet kids whose fathers beat them up and threaten them with knives, whose mothers hide bottles of vodka in the broom closet. These kids talk about the terrible things they have seen. They laugh as they brag about all the times they've poured their father's booze down the drain. I think: I don't belong here. My dad doesn't hit us and we still have money for food. Dad says he has stopped drinking forever and I believe him. He wasn't an alcoholic; he just liked his beer.

One morning I wake up early and go outside. My father's car is parked in the middle of the flower bed on our front lawn, and he's asleep in the driver's seat. A few weeks later, when my mother and I are out in the car, we find a bottle of rum in his leather briefcase in the trunk; my mother pours it out on the side of the road, cursing. I come home early from school one afternoon to find my nondrinking father with a bottle of beer in his hand and an angry, caught look on his face. He shouts at me to go away and play with my friends. Whenever I get home from school after that, I hold my breath when I turn the doorknob.

My mother tells me she has been to see a lawyer. She arranges for me to wait at a baby-sitter's house on weekdays until she gets home from work, and one afternoon she comes late to pick me up. She says my father's had an accident. I think she means in the car and start crying. Once we're home she tells me to pack a bag so that I can stay over at the baby-sitter's house that night. I see strange stains on the white carpet in our living room, more stains on the stairs leading up to my room. Blood. I find out that my father fell down the stairs and cut his head after he opened my mother's mail from the lawyer. He wasn't drinking Pepsi that day.

My mother and I leave; we come back. Things are pleasant for a while, then ugly. I despise the man who lives in our basement; his hugs and kisses make me cringe. He's sweaty and slams doors, swears and makes my mother cry herself to sleep. This man is a liar who swerves and stumbles when he walks. He falls asleep drunk, leaving pans of food burning on the stove. I think, We're going to die here. He's not my real father, I say to my mother. I use her words: *I can't take much more of this.* I tell her that I don't want to stay there, that I'll run away if she doesn't get us out soon. She hears me loud and clear, and we move into a one-bedroom apartment. The new owners of our house call the police because my father won't leave peacefully.

Yet another sort of father appears in my life. This one lives in a motel on the side of a highway, in a room crammed with things from our old house. He's three hours late for every visit and drunk when he arrives. Now that I don't have to live with him, I feel sorry for him. I know what he really means when he says he has the flu. Pity has replaced love. Sometimes it even replaces the hate. I agree to see him, even though he scares me half to death by driving past our apartment building at odd hours, looking up at our windows. I get in the car with him and try not to breathe through my nose so that I won't smell the mouthwash, or the booze under it. I beg a God I don't believe in to keep the car from crashing while I'm in it. I remember my mother shouting at my father, *If you want to kill yourself, that's one thing.*

My mother and I move to the suburbs of a nearby city with her future husband. After I graduate from high school, my mother decides to move back to my hometown; I stay in the city and begin to build a life of my own. My father comes to visit me, and we both pretend he doesn't have a drinking problem, never did. He orders Diet Coke in restaurants. Shortly after my nineteenth birthday, we go out for supper. I order a beer, and my father is startled. I enjoy the look on his face, the fear and longing. I want him to admit that he wants a drink, too, or that he had seven drinks before he came to pick me up. We keep seeing each other, keep having conversations about nothing much. I feel a vague flicker of love for him when he cries at sad movies; I am slowly recognizing the traces of my father that are present in me. We're both "too sensitive." We both cough if we laugh too hard. We both love music.

My father and I look alike, with our dark thick eyebrows and wavy hair, the same boyish jaw. But he is gaunt, with the distended stomach of the chronic alcoholic. His skin is sallow, a mix of yellow and grey that makes me burst into tears as soon as he drives away. He puts off having an operation he needs because he doesn't trust doctors. He's been in and out of hospital a few times over the years for what he seems to think are mysterious ailments. There's no mystery about it: my father is drinking himself to death. The closest I come to addressing this fact is to say "Behave yourself, Dad" when I hug him good-bye. I tell him that I'll come look after him if he decides to have the operation, that I'll clean up his apartment while he's in the hospital. A part of me is enraged that I offer this, but I do. I feel responsible for my father in a way that sickens me. He often reminds me that I am the centre of his universe, brings me groceries, and tries to make up for all the times he's let me down. I am furious with him as he limps along beside me, but something in me can't say so. On the outside I am the smiling daughter. And I am starting to forgive him, slowly, if only because I still entertain the hope that we'll have a real talk about why he threw his life away, and part of mine with it. I can feel him getting ready to tell me something when he admits he "let everything slide" after my mother and I left him.

I can drink quite a lot of beer myself by now, and I see why he likes it so much. I drink with my friends as often as I can, on every kind of occasion. I've started writing, and that gives me plenty of reasons to drink, too. I have cocktails to recover from the nervous tension of public readings, drinks to celebrate the launch of someone else's book, more drinks to console myself after being turned down by yet another magazine. My heroes are Tennessee Williams (addict, dead), Dorothy Parker (addict, dead), Raymond Carver (recovered alcoholic who died of cancer resulting from chain-smoking). My public or "literary" drinking self is not as separate from my solitary drinking self as I like to imagine. I feel increasingly lonely, whether I am surrounded by people or hidden away in my apartment with a case of beer. Like my father before me, I begin to prefer the latter. Cooking, usually one of my main passions, is now done at 3 A.M, and *gourmet* is not a word I'd use to describe the results. Breakfast is a pot of coffee and a handful of Tylenol. But I feel sure, or maybe just determined, that I'll never end up like my father. I have a job, I pay my bills, and I am never late for anything, no matter what. I follow two unspoken rules: never drink when I'm feeling sad or angry, and *never* drink at the typewriter. Drinking is something I do for fun, not because I need to. My love of beer is only that: a love of beer.

I'm working sixty hours a week in a restaurant kitchen, and yet I finally feel like my life is coming together. My second book is due out soon and I live like a real writer— drinking, smoking, and hanging out with other artists. I'm twenty-five years old and a published author, full of hope and ideas and a beautiful arrogance.

It's a busy Friday night at the restaurant where I work. The kitchen is hectic, the dining room jammed to capacity. I look forward to the end of the night, because that's when the staff sits around drinking, winding down from the chaos. As a prep cook it's my job to make sure all the chefs have what they need: chopped veggies, olive oil, minced garlic, melon balls, whipped cream. I have to hustle to keep up. The phone rings, and someone shouts that the call is for me. I give the head chef an apologetic look and stomp off to answer it.

My girlfriend and I have just broken up, so I'm surprised to hear her voice on the line. She tells me I have to call the police in my hometown right away, or my aunt. "Which aunt?" I hear myself shouting, terrified that something has happened to my mom. I haven't told either of my parents that my love life has fallen apart (again), and they don't know where to reach me. I hang up and call the friend I'm staying with, ask her to look up my aunt's number in my phone book. "You need to call your mother right away," my friend says. "What the fuck is going on?" I yell into the phone. Everyone working in the kitchen looks at me. "Your dad died," she says softly. "Please call your mom." Someone is screaming, and I realize it's me.

The chef ushers me into the back office and brings me a drink. I gulp it down, bitterly aware of the irony of this remedy. My father drank himself to death: to comfort myself I am sucking down a triple Scotch. I ask for another. Oh, well, I'm upset, I think. Who wouldn't have a drink at a time like this? I tell myself the same thing as I stop to buy a six-pack of beer on my way home. The first of my unspoken rules about drinking, Never drink when feeling sad or angry, is easily ignored. I don't know it yet, but a new rule has taken its place: *always* drink if I'm feeling either thing.

My father is now a photograph sitting on a casket. He is

clothing in a closet, dirty dishes in a sink, stacks of video cassettes and an abundant cache of frozen foods. Here but not here, just as he was throughout my childhood, only now he is absent in that most final of ways.

At the visitation and the funeral I hear countless stories about a man I had almost forgotten. It's as if the daddy who pulled the toboggan up and down the hill as many times as I asked, who laughed till tears ran down those chubby cheeks, is suddenly back in the room. He was such a nice guy, people say, a wonderful uncle. He was so passionate about helping kids. Was, used to be. What I hear breaks my heart. Something beautiful in my father had been destroyed long before his life actually ended. He was fifty-six, and it had taken him years to get what he seemed to have been looking for: the freedom to kill himself with nobody watching.

When the time comes to sort through his belongings, I refuse help from his sisters. I feel pretty certain he wouldn't like a whole bunch of people touching his stuff. I also hope—in vain—that some sort of message will present itself as I go through his trove of photographs, mementos and papers. It's a daunting task. My father wasn't just messy, he was compulsively so. He lived his last years in squalor. Upgrading from roadside motels to an apartment building in town hadn't altered his indifference to housekeeping. I work in a kind of daze as I move around the tiny basement flat trying to make sense of the chaos. It's like digging through the rubble of a bombed museum. Everywhere I turn I see evidence of the life my father once had, a life I can barely remember living with him. But among his things there isn't a single bottle of booze or beer can. I'm almost disappointed, vaguely alarmed. When my mother comes to pick me up at his building after a day of cleaning, I tell her that I think he'd finally stopped drinking. I'm painfully aware I wouldn't have believed it from him.

A few months later I rent the movie *Leaving Las Vegas*. I settle in to watch Nicholas Cage's character drink himself to death, working my way through a two-four of beer as I lament my father's early demise. There is something thrilling about this night, something dark and sad and thrilling. A sick but sweet sense of communion with my father arises.

Without being conscious of it, I begin to drink differently. I tell myself it is my father's darkness I need to understand. Night after night, I drink in the room where I keep my father's ashes, believing we are getting to know each other at last. The real us: losers both. I know it is only a matter of time before people figure out that, despite my wise-cracking exterior and seeming strength, I am my father's daughter. Frightened of everything, incapable of shrugging off the smallest disappointments, I listen to music and drink. I watch late movies and drink some more. On the nights I stand in crowded bars with friends, my thoughts are on getting back to the six-pack I've stashed in my fridge for later. I meet a version of myself I'd sworn would never exist, a pathetic creature whose survival quietly depends on cans and bottles.

My father died in March of 1996. One morning in

October 1999 I sit with my face in my hands, my head pounding from a hangover. I sit as I have on so many mornings after, wondering how and when my life became so small and dark. If this is what being an adult is all about, I think, I'd rather die. The thought startles me. I realize I can no longer continue to maintain the grand façade I grew up with: Everything is fine. Or, if it's not fine today, hell, there's always tomorrow! I look in the mirror and know that I'm a pretty dubious example of what fine looks like. Things that once gave me pleasure have ceased to do so, one by one. Who cared about getting up at sunrise anyway? Who needed stacks of clean clothes piled neatly in drawers? But the fear that I might lose my desire to do the one thing that gives me happiness—writing—sends a shudder through me. No, I think, not my words, they're all I can count on. Plenty of writers drink a lot and continue to write books—sometimes even great ones—but something in me knows I'm not up for that sort of struggle. I've tried, and it isn't working.

When I find myself sitting in a church basement surrounded by self-professed alcoholics, all I can think about is my father. I hate him for his bad example; I feel he has driven me to the same awful place. At the same time I wonder if I really need to be there. Maybe I'm just paranoid or a little undisciplined. Maybe I could still drink occasionally. I've walked into the meeting thinking that my pain is unique, that no one here will have anything to teach me because I'm an artist with a "special" set of problems. But my awareness of my father's inability to reach outside himself keeps my ass firmly planted on a folding chair when all I want to do is run. He chose to drown; I want to swim. I want a hell of a lot from life for as long as I'm meant to have it. As I listen to the people around me talk about their drinking, I know that I too am going to need some help. For the first time in my life, I ask for it.

Now, two years later, my deepest sources of strength and inspiration come not from meetings, labels or counting the number of days lived without alcohol but from writing, reading and being with friends. I've never told myself I won't *ever* have a drink again, but that, for today, I'll probably choose not to. I concentrate on how wonderful it will be to get up early with a clear head and a quiet courage I didn't know I possessed. This version of me is the one I like best so far, the one who knows she is no worse (and no better) than anyone else, her father included.

It would be great to be able to say I drank too much because my father did. It would be easy to say I drank too often because I'm a writer, and that's what real writers do. But now I think my drinking got out of control because *I wanted it to*. Initially, booze gave me an outlet, a kind of comfort I couldn't find anywhere else. But as time went on, alcohol made me more afraid, not less. The answer to my lifelong questions about my father's drinking didn't come zooming into focus as I had hoped they would. His reasons were his reasons, and I will never know what they were. I'd be lying if

I said I'm not furious and heartbroken that he isn't here now, when I've learned what I have about being alive, about drinking and drowning and all the rest of it. I wish we could have known each other as adults. But the truth is, it took his death to teach me how not to live my life. I guess that's the ultimate gift of my father's bad example, and though it's taken me years, I accept it—with both hands.

In memory of my father and for my mom, who believes in swimming.

An Open
Letter to Laura

Lois Simmie

So you've reached the Crunch. I always think of it that way, that horrible place where you know you can't drink any more and you can't not drink. It's different from the annual New Year's resolutions, or those hideously hungover declarations that made us feel so virtuous. For awhile. I stopped so many times it got embarrassing. "Are you on or off the wagon?" friends would ask, and usually I fell off in the time it took to ask the question. The Crunch. The alcoholic Big C. It's the end of the road. You know.

You've been to your first meeting of sober alcoholics, seen the faces, heard the stories. Like me at my first meeting, you were amazed that we looked so good, could laugh at ourselves, but if we only dwelled on the bad stuff there'd be no one there. And absurd things happened to alcoholics, of course. A natural-born klutz, I fell up and down stairs, in and out of cars, *under* one twice. I guess I wasn't meant to die of carbon monoxide poisoning. Or alcoholism, thank God. And neither are you.

You told us you want to stay sober more than anything. More than you want to drink, you said, and then added "almost," and everyone laughed. But that's the place we need to get to or it isn't going to happen. Hold that resolve close, Laura. Make it your mantra against the times when you're sorely tempted. You want to stay sober more than you want to drink.

As for the nitty-gritty, when your gut is tied in that knot that only a drink can fix? When a meeting is hours away, and no one answers the phone? Then you don't drink an hour at a time, a few minutes even, *just till this damn craving passes and I can think!* That long. Take deep breaths. (I'd have killed without my cigarettes.) Drink anything but booze till you slosh. Get out and walk, maybe to the library; they never offer you drinks there. And when that urge passes, quit for another hour. You're trying to save your life. Not that the grim prospect of insanity, cirrhosis or death ever stopped an alcoholic. *(Hey, it was a good liver while it lasted.)* It's the sickness of the soul that gets us.

You're heartsick about what you're doing to your children. That's sobered up more women alcoholics than anything else, I think. We love our children, and most of us didn't beat our kids, weren't maliciously cruel. We didn't break bones, we broke promises. That movie they looked forward to, but friends dropped by and we poured drinks and it was "We'll go next week, okay, honey?" And they can't say it damn well isn't okay. Or we were sick with "the flu"—that malevolent virus that unfairly attacked us more than other people—and couldn't have survived all those screaming kids at the swimming pool, doing well if we managed to get out of bed in time to make supper. Or we missed a parent-teacher interview with that same strain of flu.

But now we have the chance to try to make it up to them. Unlike my old school friend, who wouldn't or couldn't be honest with herself long enough to stay stopped. The fifteen-year-old son she loved so much found her dead in bed, her liver destroyed by cirrhosis, her skin a shocking ochre. No open casket at that funeral. A cherished, *needed* mother, who couldn't call herself alcoholic, lost to alcohol. Your children will have a mother, Laura, not just the faint memory of a woman who cried as she hugged them too tight.

It was dread of what might happen to my children that brought me to the Crunch. Did I really drive 150 miles home from Regina after drinking all night, no sleep, at eighty-five, ninety miles an hour, waking up twice heading for the ditch, the ten-year-old son I adored asleep on the back seat? I shook all that day like never before. Like I might fly apart.

And, shortly after, the obscene phone call, *I'm going to fuck your daughter*, my wild drive out to the stables, frantic to find the one not at home. I sat on a hard bench and watched her fourteen-year-old grace as she rode around and around the ring, her hair, the horse's coat shining the same reddish blonde under the light. No one else there. Vulnerable. I recognized that voice on the phone. It was the man I'd invited to share our table at a dance the night before, my husband not impressed and who could blame him? Everybody my best friend when I drank. I'd blabbed away to a total stranger: who we were, where we lived, the kids' activities, he was so interested in those. On the bench in that empty arena, I wept for what could have happened to her. For what had happened to me.

A week later I told the psychiatrist treating my depression that I thought I might have a drinking problem *(thought? might?)*, and he asked if I'd ever had a blackout. When I said, "Oh, yes" (like didn't *everybody?*), "Only alcoholics have blackouts," he informed me, and suggested where I could go for help. He looked so sorry for me. But I was elated. God, yes, I wasn't crazy! Not a bad person! Just an alcoholic! How bloody wonderful! And I still think so.

Alcoholics' stories are so similar, Laura, except for the details—my highway story; you driving drunk on a five-lane freeway to hockey practice, the kids too scared to squabble; Al telling about the flask in his briefcase that leaked all over a client's papers; your son hugging you and feeling the airline liquor bottles taped under your breasts. The young guy who came out of a blackout in another city to find his dead hamster packed in his suitcase. And my favourite, the haberdasher's son who'd thrown up, spilled wine, and fallen in the mud in an expensive wool suit and then, expecting a visit from Dad, put the suit through the washer and dryer at the laundromat. "It would have fit a monkey," he said. Stories sometimes hilarious, sometimes tragic, often moving. I'm hooked on the stories. I always have been.

The spouse who drinks too much is also familiar, and, yes, that will make it harder for you. Mine drank as much as I did, maybe more, losing his driver's licence at least twice, but he didn't call himself an alcoholic, and maybe he wasn't. He didn't suffer the guilt and remorse that became my almost constant companions, and to think I time and again invited their mean-spirited company tells you something about where I was in my life.

I'm grateful for those ghastly hangovers—the self-hatred, the bewilderment (I did it *again* in spite of my best intentions?), the awful inexplicable loneliness—that contributed to my final desperation. How can a woman sitting down as supper cooks, kids talking and playing around her, feel so alone? I didn't know that was a symptom of the illness. I loved it for so long: the warmth, the camaraderie, the silliness. "Pour me a drink, honey, it's already dark under the house." I couldn't believe it had turned mean, abusive, a love affair gone too wrong to save.

If your husband isn't happy losing his drinking partner— and some aren't—that's his problem, Laura. You won't have to remember the two of you shutting yourselves away in the den with a bottle to discuss your children's drug problems.

That one still haunts me. I can see the printed burlap curtains in the bay window seat, the wall of books and the recliner chair I escaped into, the orange shag rug that popped up crumbs like fleas when raked. Can feel the hurt silence in the rest of the house. Those silences broke my heart. They still do as I write this. The marriage ended six years after I stopped drinking. We made so many mistakes. He put making a lot of money ahead of our troubled, mixed family, and I turned more and more to alcohol, until a comfort became a crutch became an illness. One that leaves scars.

As you learn about this disease—dis-ease so true in my case; I so often drank to feel comfortable—many things will fall into place. I saw the pile of self-help books on your coffee table last night. I read dozens of those books, one after another, especially when hungover, for the flicker of hope they sometimes offered. The truth was out there. The person I wanted to be. Had maybe even been before alcohol. The only trouble was, not one of those books mentioned alcohol; how it wastes so much time, holds you back. I had always planned to write, would often put down an indifferent novel and say "I sure as hell could write a better book than that," depressed deep down that I hadn't even tried. I never wrote a thing till I put away the rye and Coke (a sophisticated drinker I wasn't) for the last time. I have twelve books out there now, a new one this fall and a finished novel ready to go. You want to go to university, Laura, become a social worker. Now it's possible.

Christmas is almost here, and that's scary as hell. The year I finally stopped I planned to wait till after the festive season but only made it to December 15. Did I say festive? Driving the wrong way down a one-way street; lying naked on the bathroom floor all night too sick to leave the toilet; in bed after God knows how many drinks, a pack and a half of cigarettes and a couple of Valium to slow the motor, feeling my heart stop for what seemed like ages, oh God, was I going to die and ruin everybody's Christmas? As festive as gangrene creeping up your leg. The booze will be flowing, so give some thought to how you want to handle that. I always say "No thanks, it makes me drunk and disorderly." They think I'm kidding.

But how did I deal with *that* Christmas? With the visiting in-laws arguing about which house to buy; the niece in her terrible twos; the husband and brother-in-law emerging from the basement only to mix more drinks; loud drum rolls from the ten-year-old's new snare drum announcing arrivals, departures and everything else. (That kid, a journalist now with books of his own, proudly told his teachers about the secret club I'd joined for people who didn't drink.)

How did I get through it? By going to a meeting Christmas Eve; putting the turkey in the oven, grabbing my coat, and heading for one Christmas Day no matter what anybody thought; going to a meeting Boxing Day. And between meetings thinking about going to one. I can still remember the happy feeling that gave me. Thank God they're never cancelled. Someone is always there to open the doors, make the coffee, listen. Because every year there are white-knuckled people like me out there just hanging on till it's time for the meeting.

Early in my sobriety I heard a crusty old guy say, "Sometimes it just takes guts," and that got me through more than one crisis. A lucky few have the obsession to drink lifted immediately. I wish. Sober a few months, I spent a night alone at the Macdonald Hotel in Edmonton. As I passed the bar on the way to the dining room, the urge became so strong I ran up three flights of stairs and locked myself in the bathroom, as if the gleaming bottles behind the bar were outside trying to get in. I filled the tub and sat there crying like a baby and blubbering that advice over and over till the craving passed and I could trust myself to order from room service. I didn't want to be a person with no guts. I had started and never finished so many things in my life. I didn't want to fail at this, too, didn't want to lose the happy feeling bubbling up as one sober day followed another. It had been so long since I'd felt that. I couldn't remember the last time I'd laughed till I cried. And one of my nicknames as a kid was Happy.

You'll develop your own strategies. One of mine had to do with my right eyelid. Toward the end, after a night of heavy drinking, it would droop so that the eye was open only about the width of a dime and, try as I might, standing in front of the bathroom mirror, I could not open it any farther. (I later read that heavy drinking can paralyze a muscle like that.) So if I had to go where drinks were served—which was everywhere, it seemed—I'd look at myself in the mirror and say, "When you come home tonight and walk, not fall, up the stairs and into the bathroom, you will look in the mirror with both eyes open and say, 'You didn't take a drink tonight, you wonderful, brave person you.'" An E.B. White essay talks about someone glimpsing, in the jungle of fear (as he had so often glimpsed before), "the flashy tailfeathers of the bird Courage." I know exactly what he meant.

At some point a sneaky little thought will probably jump into your head and whisper seductively in your ear, *Maybe you're not an alcoholic.* I heard it at a meeting in a jail, with inmates telling their horrific stories and a chairman wise enough to look at us and smile. "If anyone out there is thinking maybe you're not an alcoholic," he said, "I can assure you that social drinkers don't sit around wondering if they're alcoholics." Damn! In my head I had already poured myself a drink as soon as I got home. And quite excited I was about it, too. Speaking of social drinkers, my alcoholic friend Clint says when he tries to pour his wife and his aunt a second drink, they tell him, "Oh, no thanks, I'm beginning to feel it." *No thanks, I'm beginning to feel it???*

You aren't comfortable without your old friend Booze to soften the edges and probably won't be for a while. I remember thinking the fun was over; you know, all that fun I've been telling you about. But you know what? Living without alcohol is a very interesting experience.

You start noticing things more. Jeez, when did all those big buildings go up downtown? Odd things will make you cry, like a hole in the stocking of a small Christmas angel. You'll be struck by beauty: red flowers against a yellow wall; the arch of your black cat's neck as he washes himself; blue jays in a snowy tree—were they always that exquisite shade of blue? Those words from "Amazing Grace" say it much better than I ever could: "I once was lost, but now am found, / Was blind but now I see." I don't believe there's a recovered alcoholic who isn't affected by that song. Believe me, you're going to feel so much more, you'll have moments of wanting not to feel so damn much.

But mostly you're going to love life again. The happiness of getting through the first barbecue with your old drinking friends sober. Surviving a wild kids' birthday party without sipping from a drink in the cupboard. Discovering you can go on a holiday and enjoy yourself while everyone else still drinks. Laughing the way you used to. Just feeling good.

Your world is about to get a whole lot bigger, Laura, and I'm excited for you. Just remember what you said last night: you want to stay sober more than you want to drink.

The rest will come.

How to Quit
Smoking in Fifty
Years or Less

Peter Gzowski

As I write, the odometer on my computer for the solitaire game called Klondike has just clicked over at 13,500 hands. My ten best scores have all been rung up since June of 2000, but I started long before that, getting faster, if not better, all the time. I'm so fast now I can open the file, knock off a couple of games while I'm still thinking of how to answer an e-mail, and close it again before you'd notice. But let's say every game takes a minute. That's 13,500 minutes: 225 hours. Six thirty-five–hour weeks. Not counting research, I once wrote a book in not much more time than that.

Klondike is classic solitaire: red nine on black ten, black ten on red jack. The number of decisions you make is minuscule, and if you take a wrong turn you can have what golfers call a mulligan, press UNDO and go back. So what's the point? I have no idea. Yet without warning, I'll find myself stopping in mid-paragraph to . . . There, dammit, I've done it again. Opened the file while you weren't looking. 13,504. And if I hadn't stopped then, I might have played all morning. Many days it's as if I can't get going at the keyboard if I don't play a little Klondike first.

I'm the same with the *Globe and Mail* cryptic crossword. I'm convinced I need it to kick-start my mind. When *Morningside* went on the road in the years I was hosting it, I'd get someone to fax me the *Globe* puzzle as soon as it hit the streets in Toronto. Which would confuse my colleagues in, say, Inuvik, but keep me from twitching. At least I can understand the appeal of the cryptic—it's a contest between you and the usually anonymous puzzle-setter, and there's a pleasure in winning. There's even a kind of brother- (and sister-) hood of crypticians who nod to each other across the aisles of airplanes when they see a *Globe* opened at the appropriate page, although the quickest way to lose your membership is to dare to give someone an answer he hasn't asked you for.

And, oh, hell, I watch *Frasier*, too—every weeknight, on a channel that seems to have archived his every move since he left *Cheers*. His program comes on at 6:30 in Toronto, right after a CBC hybrid called *Canada Now*. There are worse routines of TV watching, I'm sure, and lots of less worthy expressions of U.S. popular culture than sitcoms. But I still feel out of control as I slouch deeper into my favourite chair, wave farewell to Ian Hanomansing, and tune in to the latest misadventures of a self-centred snob and his clearly unbalanced younger brother, whose nose bleeds when he fibs. If these guys are psychiatrists, no wonder we're all a little nuts. 13,506, 07, 08, 0 . . .

Klondike, cryptics, *Frasier.* Coffee (though I'll come back to that). Ritz crackers with peanut butter, going sockless until December, correcting other people's grammar, writing down phone numbers but not the names of their owners, saying "gonna," flicking mindlessly through the channels at three in the morning—all things I do but am convinced, rightly or wrongly, I could stop any time I set my mind to it. The difference between those habits, if habits they are, and what I think we mean by addictions is at least three-fold, the folds being:

1. With the possible exception of my compulsive channel hopping, I'm not hurting anyone else when I indulge in them;

2. If I were to stop playing Klondike or doing morning cryptics or baring my bony white ankles to the autumnal breezes, I would almost certainly not start shaking and retching from withdrawal; and

3. The price of continuing with these pastimes would not be death.

☞

Considering what smoking came to mean to me—there are almost no photographs of me after the age of seventeen in which I do not have a cigarette either in my hand or dangling from my lips, and no stories written about my times on radio or television without at least a mention of my lighting-one-after-the-other habit—not to mention what it means to me now, when I am pretty well confined to barracks with an oxygen tube up my nose and a four-wheeled buggy, like a baby's pram without the baby, that enables me to walk from one end of the apartment to the other . . . considering that, and all the other ways smoking and its effects have taken over my existence, it is perhaps surprising that I can't remember my first cigarette.

Of course, unless you count the time the apple-cheeked daughter of a farm family on the edge of town pinned me to the barnyard sod and brought a hitherto unknown—well, unknown in someone else's company—feeling to my loins, I can't remember the first time I had sex, either. And wherever it occurred, I'm sure my initiation to smoking was less pleasant than my barnyard romp. It still bemuses me, in fact, that something that became so hard to stop was, all those many years ago, so hard to start. I can't remember if cigarettes ever actually made me throw up—certainly my first cigars did, later on—but I can vividly recall the world spinning after a few puffs, my eyes running and my stomach heaving, as if I'd given myself the instant flu. Furthermore, cigarettes tasted awful.

So why did I start? Don't be silly. We all started. We had to. It was what you did, as much a part of approaching manhood as our cracking voices and the hair that was sprouting in all the predicted places. Girls? I'm sure they were experimenting with smoking, too, but in my memory the rites of cigarettes were as segregated as the skating rinks where we spent our winter afternoons, two rinks to a park: one, with boards, for the boys and the young men, and a second, with snowbanks, for the little kids, the sissies and the figure-skating girls.

If I smoked corn silk or any other boyhood imitations of tobacco, I don't remember doing it. I don't know where I would have learned. *Chums* or *The Boy's Own Annual*, which steered me through everything from the rules of cricket to the best way to make papier-mâché puppets (you model the head over a Vaseline-smeared light bulb) would have been no help, and Ernest Thompson Seton, my guide to all things natural, had other matters on his mind. So my smoking cronies and I found ways to come up with tailor-mades, though I didn't learn to call them that until much later. We filched them from our mothers' purses and our fathers' dressers or scrounged them from older siblings or, when flush with our allowances or snow-shovelling money, bought them ourselves, telling the shopkeeper, if he cared—and no one seemed to— that we were running an errand for someone else. Players, Export A, Buckingham, Turret, Sweet Caporal, Winchester, Sportsman (with its drawings of fishing flies on the yellow package) or, exotically, the menthol-flavoured Kools. We tried them all, discussing their various merits. We smoked furtively, cupping our hands around the glowing embers as we passed our elders on the streets, proud of our increasing ability to inhale without coughing.

☞

It's clear, I trust, that I am not yet talking about an addiction. A pastime, maybe. Something to do, always in and with company. We were social smokers, lighting up not because of how it made us feel, which was still more often queasy than high, but of how we wanted the rest of the world to see us— grown-up, cool (if that catchall adjective had begun to trickle down from the remote world of jazz), downtown. "I'm dying for a cigarette," we would whisper conspiratorially to each other at Friday evenings' Teen Canteens, when what we were really dying for was a break from the self-consciousness of dancing. But if cigarettes had disappeared from the face of the earth overnight, the extent of our withdrawal symptoms would have been a disappointed "Aw, shit, what'll we do now?"—not unattached, I'd say, to a certain sense of relief.

A lifetime later, when people who loved me or were worried about me or, in some cases, were paid a lot of money to figure out why I persisted in a habit that was so clearly shortening my days among them, would ask me why I didn't quit, I could sometimes do no better than "I smoke because I smoke." In the absence of a reason not to—a municipal bylaw, a coughing child, a disapproving hostess, the knowledge that an open flame might blow me and everyone in the room to kingdom come—it was simply a lot easier to light up than to forbear. Unless I consciously stopped myself from doing so, I smoked. Even when I was sucking back three large packages a day—seventy-five cigarettes, which is about as many as you can get through if you're still going to sleep a few hours—there were very few that I actually decided to smoke. The first one in the morning, sure, though that was more a reflex than an act of free will, my hand reaching across the alarm clock before my feet were ready to hit the floor, and the last one at night. A cigarette after each meal or task completed, and certain others through the day—to pick myself up, to relax, to sharpen my appetite or ease the pangs of hunger. But most of the time, I smoked without thinking, often not realizing I had lit a cigarette until I noticed it burning in the ashtray. Would I have gone into withdrawal if I'd stopped then? Absolutely. Even the first hour of a transcontinental flight would have me drumming my fingers and looking at my watch, and on the rare occasions I could be talked into going to a nonsmoking restaurant or accepting an invitation to a house with no ashtrays, I seldom made it to dessert without having to go for a walk. Over the years, I never really gave the storm clouds of abstinence time to gather. I just lit another cigarette.

My mother smoked Winchesters. She was the most glamorous woman not only in my life but in the whole of Galt, so far as I was concerned, if not the entire western world. She was a divorcée, the daughter of a well-to-do Toronto lawyer (or well-to-do until 1929, at least), alumna of a Toronto private girls' school, a Swiss lycée and a British university, still not quite thirty when she remarried into small-town Presbyterian Ontario, by day the children's librarian and by night a willowy star of both mixed-doubles badminton and such Galt Little Little Theatre productions as Noel Coward's *Blithe Spirit.*

My father had smoked Winchesters too, before he'd left for Depression-era vagrancy and, eventually, war. Their marriage lasted not much longer than a couple of flat fifties, barely time enough for me to pop onto the scene in 1934. Margaret, as the world called her, struggled for a while as a single mother in Toronto after divorcing my vagabond father and then—largely, I've always been convinced, so I'd have an untroubled home to grow up in—married Reg Brown of Galt, Ontario, who was the sales manager of a local textile mill and, because of a childhood ear injury, ineligible for war.

Galt, a prosperous city of some 18,000 on the Grand River (it has since been absorbed into the much larger Cambridge), was an idyllic place to be a kid. I was five when we moved there. We lived in an upper duplex overlooking Dickson Park, home of the Galt Terriers of the Intercounty Baseball League and site of both the annual fall fair and the skating rinks that were the centre of my childhood winters. It was an easy bicycle ride down Water Street to my mother's daytime headquarters on the second floor of the Carnegie library and to the hustle and bustle of a busy market town, with its principal intersection—Main and Water—marked by four imposing banks, one to a corner. But just as convenient in the other direction were the deciduous woods, murmuring streams and stone-fenced farmlands of pastoral Waterloo County.

As clear a memory as any I have of boyhood is the winter day of *verglas*, when a soft overnight rain was snap-frozen on top of a county-wide bed of snow. With the sun glittering off the land, the puck from our morning hockey game skittered over the boards. As we chased it, the blades of our skates skimmed across the frozen veneer. We took off, first out to the edge of the park, then hopping the fence, skates and all, out onto Blair Road and across the rolling farmscape, slaloming into the valleys, sidestepping up the hills, gliding across pastures and fallow fields, as free, for that one sparkling day, as the gulls that soared over the riverbanks. It was, as I say, the perfect place to be a boy.

"You smoke, don't you?" my mother said one day when I was fourteen, apropos, so far as I could tell, of nothing.

"Well, sort of. I . . ."

"Peter?"

"Yes. Yes, I do, actually."

I can see her still, clad in her slip, sitting at her dressing table's triptych of mirrors in the sunny bedroom she shared with my stepfather. We often talked there. I would perch on one of the twin beds as she finished her makeup for an evening out, tried on a piece of her family jewellery, or stained her long legs a silken brown, carefully painting a faux seam from her heel to the back of her knees. Later, I would come to realize how troubled she was in those times, how penned in she had come to feel in Galt and by her second marriage, but if there were signs of it in our early-evening chats, they were not discernible by my adolescent antennae. I loved my times alone with her, and she, I think, took pleasure in my company. She would tell me tales of her childhood summers on her father's hobby farm or of her schooling in Europe or, sometimes, if Reg were not around, of how kind my father's family had been to her after he had left his fledgling marriage—and his fledgling—to seek his fortune. On the rare occasions we actually talked about my father, she took pains not to criticize him. "You remind me of him," she would say from time to time, echoing observations I'd often heard from my Gzowski grandparents.

On the matter of my smoking, I think she was more amused than angry, maybe even secretly pleased that I had taken another step on the road to manhood and independence. "Look," she said, "if you're going to do it, you don't have to sneak around." She opened the pale-blue package with its red and gold lettering, pushed up the tip of a Winchester, and held it out toward me. "Here," she said, smiling, and reached for her Ronson lighter.

☙

Does anyone honestly believe we didn't know smoking was bad for us? We may not have realized it would eventually kill us, or suspected it could rock us back on our heels the way I'm now rocked—I have what the health care system, bless its heart, calls COPD, for Chronic Obstructive Pulmonary Disease, but which everyone knows really means emphysema, just as acne really means boils and pimples. We probably hadn't heard of lung cancer or considered the devil's catalogue of other afflictions the world now understands are caused by smoking. But everyone knew that cigarettes did something different to your body than, say, asparagus. "That'll stunt your growth," people would say. Or "Sounds like a smoker's cough to me." Danger? If we'd even admitted there was any—a difficult concession to pry from a teenager about anything—it would only have added to the allure.

No, I'm afraid I can't pass the buck for my weakness quite as easily as do the people who've been launching class-action suits. Good luck to them, I guess. I have no sympathy for anyone who works for the merchants of death the tobacco companies have turned out to be, and if lawsuits help to put them out of business, then so much the better. But tobacco companies and their shills didn't start me on the path to the oxygen tent. I'd no more think of suing them than I'd think of suing Humphrey Bogart.

I left Galt the next year. I was screwing up in high school, a better pool shot than a Latin scholar, miserable at home. During the Christmas break of Grade 11, I went to Toronto to look up my father. With some reluctance, for he was working on a new relationship at the time, he took me in, then packed me off to Ridley College, his old boarding school in St. Catharines.

Smoking was a caning offence at Ridley, which was proud of its football teams. The penalty was ten painful whacks across the rump delivered by the headmaster. Legend had it, though no one made the roster during my time there, that the most exclusive society in the school was the "Armchair Club," whose entry requirements were ten times ten strokes of the cane. I didn't come close to qualifying. The only time I would ever feel the sting of the cane at Ridley was following an episode in which my entire Grade 12 class slipped out one night, climbed aboard a secretly chartered bus, and made our way across the river to the iniquitous United States. We were caught trying to sneak back into school, our heads spinning and our boasts of how drunk we were echoing in the midnight air. But there was a certain panache about defying the smoking law, and in due course I learned how to smear toothpaste onto my gums to mask the smell, how to dry loose tobacco on a dormitory radiator, and, most enterprising of all, how to steam up the communal shower in the basement of our residence so I could stand near the back wall, naked as a kewpie doll, and smoke a cupped cigarette down to its soggy dregs.

In the first summer after I'd been at Ridley, my mother died. She was thirty-nine. She was buried in Galt, and my father came to the funeral. He still smoked Winchesters, I noticed. I went back to school in the fall, and though I remember little of the next year, with the compulsory study sessions every evening my marks started to go up. In my graduating year, I made the first football team and stopped smoking for the season. But a broken hand suffered in practice ended my career. As soon as I could get back into that basement shower, draping a towel over the plaster cast that covered my wrist and hand, I lit up again. By the time I enrolled at university the next fall—on a couple of scholarships, thanks to Ridley's discipline—I was pretty well hooked.

If you're going to quit, people would advise me, you should first try to cut out the things you associate with smoking. Well, sure, I would think, except in my case I'd have to cut out waking up in the morning, going to the bathroom, having coffee, answering the phone, driving my car, writing, talking on the radio, playing board games—or even golf—meeting strangers, watching television, having a drink, finishing sex (how else do you know when it's over, I used to joke, not knowing that the smoking itself would eventually look after that) or going to sleep at night.

Winchesters, brand of my youth, went off the market. I switched to Buckinghams, another unfiltered blend that was a perennial leader on the charts of tars and other poison ingredients. I stayed with them for a long time. That was a

Buckingham people saw me light up on the final evening of my late-night TV career in the '70s ("What are they going to do, fire me?") and a Buckingham I stubbed out in an ashtray in the office of Avie Bennett, the former president of McClelland and Stewart. Avie, a militant antismoker, had practically ordered me to smoke in his office one day. When I finished, he said, "There, I have butts from the only three people I've ever let smoke in my office—you, Mordecai Richler and René Lévesque."

Once, in the early '80s, I was interviewing the artist A. J. Casson in a radio studio in Toronto. He saw my cigarettes on the table.

"Did you know I designed that package?" he asked.

"No," I said.

"During my commercial design period," he said. "A lot of us did that."

I still have that Buckingham package, open, signed and mounted in a red shadow box over the desk where I write— my only original Group of Seven.

You can't buy Buckinghams now. I switched to Rothmans when Buckinghams followed Winchesters out of business years ago.

You can't smoke in radio studios now either—or in movies, waiting rooms, limos, lobbies, university classrooms, barber shops, hockey rinks, offices, restaurants—even, for God's sake, in a lot of pool rooms and bars. I was in Yellow-knife, the last of the frontier capitals, when they outlawed smoking in government buildings. On my last day there, I asked a couple of German tourists how they liked the town.

"Fine," they said, "except for the prostitution."

"Prostitution?" I said. "In *Yellowknife?*"

"Sure," they said. "All those women standing on the sidewalk, smoking and looking up and down the street for customers."

"They're government clerks," I said. "On a smoke break."

By the time smoking had fallen out of fashion—in what has been, surely, one of the revolutionary social changes of our day—nearly all of my friends had quit. One by one, they fell by the wayside, driven not only by the now unavoidable realization that it was going to kill them but by a variation of the peer pressure that had got so many of us started in the first place. If smoking had once been smart, it was now stupid. You didn't brag about it; you were, if anything, ashamed. And what with constantly trying to figure out where you could go and when, depending on whether you could smoke or not, it was becoming more trouble than it was worth. It was, not to put too fine a point on it, a pain in the ass.

Yet still I smoked. My teeth were yellow and my fingers brown. My clothes stank and so, I'm sure, did my breath. There were holes in my sweaters and scars on my furniture. My computer keyboard was regularly choked with ashes. My car looked and smelled as if there'd been an all-night poker game in the front seat. Once, sheltering a cigarette in my pocket (shades of Ridley), I set fire to a favourite windbreaker, and more than once, holding a phone to my ear, I caught the acrid smell of burning hair. In 1996, now in my sixties, I went into hospital for surgery to fix an abdominal aortic aneurysm. About four days into my recovery, a night nurse, the one who used to prowl the halls on in-line skates, asked if I'd like to get out of bed and go downstairs with her for a cigarette, joining that sorry gaggle of people outside every hospital who lean on their IVs, bare bums exposed to the winds, as they suck on the toxin that put them there in the first place. "Are you *kidding?*" I snorted. But my first day home, with the physical craving presumably under control, I pawed through my cupboards until I found a half-full package of stale Rothmans and lit up in the living room.

Why? I still can't answer. If anyone asked, and they did, all the time, I'd say I hated my habit. It's hard to duck the fact that I probably hated myself for being such a slave to it. The reasons may well be buried in the childhood I've sketched so roughly here, but if they are, it will take a sharper brain than mine to ferret them. Whatever pleasure had once been associated with pulling the little red tab to remove the cellophane wrapping, taking out the layer of silver paper over half the package (we used to save that paper during the war so the RCAF could foil the enemy radar), pushing out the first cigarette, tapping it lightly on a table, lighting it, and then sucking that first, biting, all-engulfing, twitch-stopping drag of the day deep, deep into your lungs: whatever pleasure had once been there had long since gone. I smoked, as always, because I smoked.

At 9:30 on the morning of February 7, 2000, I pulled into the parking lot of a four-storey building in the suburbs of Toronto, rolled down the window of my ashtray on wheels, and flicked the butt of my last Rothmans into a snowbank.

After half a century of smoking, I had elected to incarcerate myself where I might find help. I'd signed on at a privately funded institution that had begun by working with alcoholics and, over the years, had grown into a treatment centre for people with addictions that varied from gambling to hard drugs to eating disorders. I'm preserving its anonymity because privacy is what the Slammer, as I came to call it, provided me, as it did all its patrons, and I feel I owe it that in return. As well, perhaps, as my life.

I'd sort of tried to quit before. Under the guidance of a wise and caring GP, into whose hands I'd been lucky enough to fall after my surgery, I experimented with Zyban, the patch, hypnosis, audiotapes, acupuncture, therapy—whatever was going. Everything worked and nothing worked. My guardian GP looked up the patch in the literature, saw how many people were having heart attacks caused by smoking while they were on it, and warned me never, ever to light up while I was attached; I ripped the patch off and had a cigarette. Hypnosis, for all my skepticism (or arrogance, if you want to be picky— of course *I* could never be hypnotized) actually took hold momentarily; I nodded off in the subject's chair while the doctor murmured soothing words and came awake to find my hand rising involuntarily at his command. But I lit up in the car on the way home and never went back. And so on. I foiled every attack. The truth was my heart wasn't in it, and the more I danced around, kidding myself and others, the better I understood the essential truth of smoking cessation: you can spend thousands on personal therapy and professional guidance, or you can stick a carrot in your ear and whistle "Four Strong Winds"—if you still have enough breath. The method makes no difference. If you've decided to quit, you will; if you haven't, you should get your affairs in order.

I was in pretty rough shape as I climbed out of my car that February morning. My drinking, another family trait, had been heavy enough for the last couple of years that it probably would have qualified me for the Slammer on its own. I was wobbly of stride, red of eye and shaky of hand. When I was introduced to the physician who would later turn out to be of particular help with my various demons, I shook his hand and, settling into the chair beside his desk, asked if he preferred to be called "Michael" or "Doctor."

"Steven will do," he said, "since that's my name."

I cannot say enough about the help—physiological as well as spiritual—I received in the Slammer, nor about the support of the people and systems I have leaned on since. I stayed inside my suburban minitower for most of a month, tranquilized through the worst of the physical withdrawal, a fresh strong patch glued daily to my flesh, making it through the nights with sleeping pills. I tried meditation and wished I were better at it, attended lectures on dependency, and went to AA meetings, where, though I resisted the air of evangelism, I found strength in facing my own weaknesses—yes, I was an addict, powerless without help. Some of the wisdom, I think, began to seep through. I made friends with a sprightly menagerie of other addicts in the Slammer, not only the predictable range of problem drinkers but also teenage druggies (some of whom, I'm sad to say, seemed to know more about the chemistry of artificial euphoria than the professionals who gave us our lectures), disarming gamblers and a bevy of extraordinarily attractive young women who would eat with us in the dining hall, a dietitian at their side, and then, if no one stayed with them, go upstairs and purge themselves to starvation.

I liked all my fellow passengers, although some of my affection may just have been the companionship of shared frailties. However stupid their behaviour, I came to think, drunks and hopheads are often clever people. A twenty-year-old heroin addict, a promising athlete who'd been the apple of her father's eye until she wrecked her knees and lost an American university scholarship, beat me at chess the first time she played me. A burly NCO from the Armed Forces, whom I initially had to coach on the finer points of Scrabble, scored two triple-triples on me in a single game.

My favourite fellow inmate was a jolly woman who had gambled away both her career and her house at the video terminals of the casinos. Hitting bottom, she'd reached such a state of despair that she staged an "armed robbery" on her local convenience store with a toy pistol, hoping that the cops would come and gun her down. But when I met her she was full of the strength she'd found in the Slammer, a dedicated Scrabble enthusiast, a passionate reader and the soul of kindness. She still faced a charge of armed robbery (it was later dismissed), but her real fear was that she'd wander one day into a provincial gambling den and be seduced not by the chance of winning her losses back—she was far too intelligent to think that was possible—but by the flashing lights and the unadulterated lure of excitement.

I had a special feeling, too, for the kids with eating disorders. Almost everyone else in the Slammer could be separated from their temptations—there were no cards in the common room, lest the gamblers succumb to pinochle for quarters, and anyone out on a day pass was liable to face a blood test on return—but everyone, including the young bulimics, had to face food every day. I would think of them after breakfast, as I watched my Scrabble partners and companions in group therapy step outside the swinging doors to smoke in the winter air, while I stayed inside.

Yet something worked. Gradually, and with a lot of help, I realized that I really did want to quit. By the time I was ready to retrieve my car from the parking lot (friends had arranged to have it taken away, vacuumed and returned ash-free), I felt like an ex-smoker. I'm still paying the price for my years of transgression. The emphysema—sorry,

COPD—that now dominates my life didn't really strike until I'd been out for a few months and was hit by a chest infection. I've had rehab for that, too, in a different kind of institution, and I work on getting better every day. It's a long haul. But a year and many thousands of games of Klondike after I tossed out that last cigarette butt, I haven't smoked again.

Oh, yes, I said I had a point to make about coffee. It's something else I learned in the Slammer. I'd been drinking coffee at least as long as I'd been smoking when I checked in. I *knew* I was addicted to caffeine, that I couldn't possibly start the day without a jolt, the stronger the better. When, as my recovery began, my hands finally stopped shaking enough for me to get a cup of coffee to my lips, all I could say was, "Thank God, now I feel human again." I kept that up every day till I got paroled. I was on my way out the door before someone told me it had been decaf all along.

More and
More

Evelyn Lau

When did it begin? The sensation of a depthless hole opening up inside me, a cavernous feeling of need. The surrendering to compulsion, which was like getting on a treadmill and not being able to get off. The craving for perfection, so that if I slipped and had one of something "bad," then the day had fallen into disarray, and I had to keep having another and another until the darkness fell.

It began in childhood, innocently. My normal child's greed for candy magnified until it became all-consuming, until the thought of the next candy crowded out every other thought in my mind—though there was little pleasure in eating it beyond the first sweet jolt on the tongue. After that moment it could have been soap or sawdust, but the urge to consume grew in me as steadily as an anxiety attack. The craving was compounded by secrecy, fuelled by being forbidden; this was the most direct route I could see to escaping the control my mother exerted over me, to sabotaging her constant vigilance. Eating surreptitiously was a way of rebelling, of declaring my body my own. I chewed smuggled sweets in bed, tossing the wrappers into the darkness behind the nearby sofa until one day, to my mortification, my father pulled the furniture away from the wall to vacuum and found the dusty, crumpled evidence. I disowned responsibility the way only a child could, claiming I didn't know how the wrappers could have gotten there, it had nothing to do with me.

Once, very early on, this desire for more must have had something to do with pleasure. Once I must have enjoyed a piece of cake or a scoop of ice cream and only wanted more of that enjoyment. But I can no longer remember such a time. I remember instead the growing panic, the desperate need that was a kind of clawing inside me. My quest for satiation blotted out everything in its path. When I was caught stealing a chocolate bar at a local drugstore, my mother screamed and hit at me wildly the moment I came home—was the food she cooked not good enough for me? Did I want people to think she was starving me? I had stolen two chocolate bars that day, but the store detective, emptying out my schoolbag, had found only one—the other had slipped between the pages of a textbook and lodged there. I hid the second bar in a drawer that afternoon, eager to get rid of it but unable to throw it away. The next day I shoved pieces of it into my mouth, fearful and ashamed, chewing miserably until it was gone. The chocolate was dark, it was bitter, it tasted like despair.

I hid sweets in my desk drawers, between the pages of books, even sometimes tucked inside my underwear when I came home from school, so that when my mother searched my pockets for contraband she would come up empty-handed. The food I ate became one of the few things my parents could not always supervise. Whenever they left me alone in the house I hurried to the orange kitchen as soon as I heard the door close behind them. Heart racing, palms sweaty, I ransacked the cupboards, consuming bits of food—a biscuit, a handful of nuts, a mouthful of whisky—that I hoped would not be missed. My mother had begun keeping meticulous track of the food in the house and forcing me every week onto the bathroom scale, which had the opposite effect of what she wanted. I was twelve, thirteen, humiliated by her mocking comments as she peered at the dial on the scale; though I was never more than ten pounds overweight, I must have seemed impossibly fleshy next to her own ninety-pound frame. When she asked me to undress, when she slapped my thighs or pinched my waist or criticized my large breasts, I detached in my mind the same way I would years later when strangers ran their hands over my body. I dreaded these intrusions, and my compulsive behaviour grew in direct proportion to her increasingly frantic efforts to monitor every aspect of my life.

Sometimes I would scurry down to the basement, where I would scoop up spoonfuls of sugar from the sacks in storage, gagging on the crystals lining my tongue. From my mother's purse I stole dimes and quarters that bought greasy paper bags of day-old cookies and doughnuts from the bakery on the way home from school. I still remember the taste of two dozen stale shortbread cookies consumed in a matter of blocks, the thick buttery dust of them in my throat, the nausea that pressed up inside me. I remember hiding behind a tree to finish the cookies before turning the corner onto the block where we lived, cramming them into my mouth; within moments I had reached a sugar and carbohydrate plateau where the clamour inside me dulled and my head felt thick, dazed. The storm of anxiety, of helpless rage, had passed for the time being. The frustration of never being good enough, of knowing I could never please my parents by winning a scholarship to medical school, of realizing that the life they wanted for me was not one I was capable of living. This happened day after day, bags of candies and pastries tearfully choked down along the corridor of streets between school and home. An hour later I would have to eat dinner, feeling so full I could hardly breathe, and that night in bed I would vow never to binge again; the next day I would wake up and be perfect at last.

But the next day I would wake in darkness, not perfect at all, and I knew I would do it again. I was driven by something larger than myself, some force I could hardly explain, let alone fight against. The tension that filled our household after my father lost his job, my mother's obsessive calibration of groceries and finances, my parents' expectations for my future . . . These things overpowered me and somehow manifested themselves in my need to keep eating until I was physically incapable of continuing.

It was as if I were trying to reach someplace that didn't exist, except in sleep or death. A perfect blankness, a white light. The search for this obliteration began with food, but later it wouldn't matter if it was food or alcohol or drugs or sleeping with men for money—the feeling was the same one I'd had as a child behind the shut door of my bedroom, gobbling up one candy, barely tasting it, so I could reach for the next, and the next. The urge was to keep going until the anxiety and rage stopped, until as a teenager I threw up or passed out or felt so blank that I no longer was myself.

⌒

One afternoon when I was sixteen or seventeen, years after I had run away from home, I sat sullenly in my psychiatrist's office with my parents. I wore a leather jacket and a miniskirt and was barely able to look at them across the room, my father's face lowered in pain and bewilderment, my mother twisting the strap of her purse between her thin fingers. My doctor was coaxing my father into telling me that he loved me.

"Chinese people don't talk about these things," my father tried to explain, haltingly. "It's not our tradition. But she knows. My wife—her mother—even when we couldn't afford any food, she would always have a cup of hot water waiting for her when she came home from school."

"She needs to hear you say it, Dad. Can you look at her and tell her?"

In a moment of what, even then, I knew was bravery worthy of a medal, my father lifted his face and looked straight at me. "Of course I love you," he said.

That was a moment I would remember from the session, though at the time I stared back at him hard-eyed. Also his mention of the hot water, how I winced at the pathos of that, and how my mother clutched my arm as my parents left the doctor's office and tried to persuade me to come home with them for dinner. Was it so simple as food equalling love? Was it their love I was after, in all the years of my life when I threw one thing after another into that bottomless well, and all of those things—food, drugs, alcohol, men—simply fell in and disappeared? What happened in the beginning that caused this? Something my mother did when I was an infant at her breast? Did she not come when I cried, did she hold me too tightly or turn her back when she should have stayed? Was there a chemical deficiency in my brain, a lack of serotonin, a predisposition toward these moods and impulses and compulsions? Was it a milder version of the mental illnesses that had stunted the lives of several of my mother's sisters, consigning them to a lifetime of antipsychotic medications and hospitals? Was it nature or nurture, creation or circumstance?

One substance replaced another, changing with the seasons. I gave up food for drugs, cigarettes for alcohol, moved fluidly back and forth, tried various combinations. As a teenager it was marijuana, LSD, tranquilizers, painkillers and cocaine. I binged on these drugs, finding a more complete oblivion through chemicals, a more extensive loss of self, of memory and pain. Candy is dandy, but liquor is quicker . . . and nothing is so quick as a few lines of white glitter, a syringe dripping with a morphine derivative. Even when the acid gave me bad trips, even when the world morphed into a greater nightmare than it already seemed, being high was still better than staying inside myself. I sought through drugs to be somebody else—anybody else.

At nineteen, when I stopped smoking three packs of cigarettes a day, I began my mornings instead with a drink in hand. That drink led to another and another, as the day devolved and the sun spiralled down in the sky. I no longer used street drugs, but started to mix alcohol with the prescription tranquilizers—Halcion, Ativan, Xanax—I obtained from various men, including the middle-aged married psychiatrist with whom I had a destructive yearlong affair. Twenty was a lost year, a calendar of blackout evenings, mornings where I could remember nothing of what I had said or done the night before, or how I had gotten home in the end. When I stopped taking pills, the bulimia that had come and gone in earlier times became one long unbroken stretch of binging and purging. I was throwing up seven or eight times a day and spending nearly as much on food as I had on drugs or alcohol.

Once, in my early twenties, I went out for lunch with two of my aunts. I was hungover from the night before. I could barely touch the greasy dim sum, and I lost my temper when one of them kept insisting that I eat. When we were ready to leave, I said I'd wait for them outside while they used the washroom. A few minutes later I changed my mind and went to use the bathroom myself; as soon as I opened the door I could hear them talking about me behind the closed doors of their stalls.

"I know why she's the way she is," one aunt declared, in Chinese. "It's not her fault. Her mother stayed in bed too long when she was pregnant, she didn't move around enough. I think it did something to Evelyn's brain, that's why she's like this. She can't help it, she's disturbed . . ."

I turned on my heel and slammed the door on my way out, enraged. How dare she assume there was something wrong with me? I refused to believe it myself. Yet that was how my whole family had dealt with my running away and becoming involved in drugs and prostitution—I was "mentally ill," which, in an odd way, absolved me of blame and responsibility. Once, to my psychiatrist's amusement, he received a phone call from this aunt, who insisted that I must be hearing voices; it was the only explanation for my behaviour. In her way, she believed I was pure, that none of it was my choice, that no one sane would choose such a life.

⁀

Was it a choice? Many people believe addicts are weak, that their suffering stems from a lack of willpower, that an addiction or a dependency can be overcome by strength of character alone. Intellectually I lean toward this belief as well, but emotionally it is a different story. I think of how many people would like to have more than one cookie out of the bag they bring home from the supermarket. Some of them do have several cookies, savouring them, then place the rest of the bag in the cupboard. Others have a harder time doing that; they eat too many cookies, half the package perhaps, then feel repentant and disgusted with themselves. But imagine ratcheting that urge up further. Imagine that you are unable to sleep because of the cookies in your cupboard, that you can't work or read or leave the house knowing the uneaten cookies are there. That a feeling of anxiety begins to build in you, a desperation and a kind of anger, until you break down and cram the cookies into your mouth several at a time, devouring them until you throw up. If, after you throw up, there are still some cookies left in the bag, you have to keep eating them, even though by then you are sick of their taste and texture. If there are ten bags of cookies and no way that you can eat them all, you will have to bury the rest of them immediately at the bottom of the garbage pail—first crushing them and soaking them in water, say, to prevent your retrieving them later—in order to be rid of them.

Is this behaviour something that can be changed by force of will? The feelings behind that scenario: what are they? Are they symptoms of some other hunger, some emotional lack or faulty wiring in the brain? I don't know, but I have lived with those feelings, those uncontrollable impulses, all my life.

I don't like the word "addiction." It conjures up dismal pictures of sober or lapsed strangers sitting together talking about their dependencies week after week, year after year, mired in the language of abstinence and recovery. I find myself impatient with people who identify themselves so closely with their affliction. There is something in me that scorns the weak-chinned, bleary-eyed, sad-sack faces of recovering addicts whose lives and vocabulary have been overtaken by their illness. And yet the emotions they cycle through, the force that dictates their behaviour, must not be so different from mine.

Sometime toward my mid-twenties, the fog began to clear. Your body tires, your life changes, you climb out of the whirlpool and onto dry land. Certainly there were still days when I ate or drank to the point of vomiting, there were unhealthy relationships to become obsessed with, but I didn't lose myself in the same way any more. With adulthood came the knowledge that emotions and experiences that seemed decimating at the time would pass, and sooner rather than later. I was no longer always facing the end of the world.

I became like everyone around me, with a mortgage and RRSPS and responsibilities, and if there were nights when I went out and drank too many martinis or glasses of wine, then stayed up all night throwing up in the bathroom—well, who didn't?

Now I'm almost thirty, the once unimaginable age. "Time to give up childish things," my psychiatrist chides. Once in a while I still binge and purge, but one lapse no longer triggers a six-month cycle as it used to. I often eat too much to quell some anxiety or emptiness, but now I can usually stop it from escalating into the sort of frenzy that leads to forced vomiting. Sometimes I drink vast quantities of alcohol and lose myself, but this is no different from the behaviour of many people I know. It's never a problem for me to have only one glass of wine at dinner, or to keep alcohol around the apartment without consuming it, or to go for days without a drink. Illegal drugs haven't interested me for a decade, and pills— well, there are vials of tranquilizers in my drawer that have lain there untouched for eight years. But a little part of me is still glad when I get a headache. Even the small amount of codeine in several Tylenol 1's makes me feel more confident and slightly elevated. So, after all these years of almost never taking a sleeping pill or a painkiller, I must still be cautious. The old desire for oblivion is not gone, only lying dormant, as are the temptation to slip into sleep rather than live through a difficult emotion and the longing to give in. And yet I know that if I give in, the next day will be harder as a result. That in the morning the previous day's anxiety, temporarily muffled by pills, will be back—tripled, quadrupled. That my hands will shake, my nerves will be frayed, and I will be less armoured than before.

The compulsions, the feelings of need and lack, are still there. They are always there. At one time, it was worth any price to get away from them—to feel bright and confident, to find the clearing in the forest where the sun streamed down and I was complete. I think now that these urges will stay with me for the rest of my life. The feelings will ebb and flow; maybe one day things will be a lot easier, and maybe they won't. At least I no longer wake up every morning expecting to be perfect, then destroying myself if I am not. Though I would never have believed it as a teenager, you do move beyond things, outgrow the person you were. Sometimes, just by staying alive, you find you have become someone who can live in the world after all.

Breathing
under Ice

Lorna Crozier

It's dark in the back yard. Around eleven o'clock. Flashlight in hand, clad in my red flannelette nightgown, I search through the thick ivy around the trellis near the door, then in the woodpile and in the tin shed where we keep the lawn mower, garden tools and wheelbarrow. I've already gone through the shelves in the back of the bedroom closet, the dresser drawers, the filing cabinets, the laundry basket, the high kitchen cupboard that I can't reach without a stool. Outside, my bare feet getting cold, I move faster from place to place, afraid Patrick will rise from bed where he's been the past hour, turn on the porch light, and ask what I am doing. I pull the lever and flip the driver's seat of his truck forward, and there it is—the vodka bottle gleaming in the flashlight's narrow beam.

I feel elated. Charged. Vindicated. All afternoon I had

thought he was drinking. Though I smelled nothing on his breath, there was that look around his eyes, the sideways shift of attention that feels as if a thin film of water has slipped between us and slightly distorted the way we engage. It's never anything I can be sure of, nothing I can put my finger on. He could just be tired, he could be distracted, he could be in the middle of dreaming himself into a poem. "Have you been drinking?" I finally asked. "No," he replied. But now I have the evidence: the fact of a cold, almost empty twenty-sixer in my hand.

I want to throw it at the moon, I want to pour the colourless liquid over the driver's seat and drop a lighted match, I want to carry the bottle inside, shake Patrick by the shoulder, and shout "Look what I've found!" Instead I tuck the bottle back in its hiding place and sit on the step, my head in my hands, wondering how in the world, at fifty years old, I've ended up here.

⁀

There's a photograph of my dad and me the night of my Grade 12 graduation. I'm in my first long dress, a sleeveless, aqua peau-de-soie with small covered buttons spilling down the right side. For the first time in my life, I have a hairdo. Ginnie at the local shop has shaped my curls into a bundle of sausage rolls on top of my head. Later I'll groan every time I look at my hair in this photo. Now I think it's as sophisticated as anything I'd see in a *Movietone* magazine.

Dad is wearing his only suit. It's the same kind most prairie men of his background and generation save for weddings and funerals, ignoring the shifts in fashion or their body shape. His arm drapes across my shoulders and, as he turns from me to the camera, his sloppy grin looks as if it's about to slide off his face. Before Mom snaps the picture, he says, "You're my little girl."

In the photograph our feet don't show. Mine are in satin high heels dyed the same colour as my dress. He's wearing his good oxfords, as they were called. Mel Caswell's wife gave them to him when Mel died. They were both small men with small feet, but every time Dad wears the shoes he complains that they pinch. If you could see the oxfords in the photograph, you'd notice that the laces are undone. After the picture, Mom, in a snit, sits Dad on the couch, yanks the laces, and knots a bow. He leans on her as we walk to the door.

We're close to being late for the banquet in the school gym a few blocks away. We *have* to be on time; I'm the valedictorian and my family is supposed to sit with the principal at the head table, where I'll give my speech after everyone's consumed the ham, scalloped potatoes and jellied salads. Over coffee and apple pie, my fellow grads and their parents will listen to my optimistic, conservative lines about the values our elders have taught us and how these will guide us through the years to come. There's no sense of teenaged angst, no disrespect or rebellion in my speech, no true words about what I've learned from my father. Though it's 1966, it's small-town Saskatchewan, and "the Sixties" are happening somewhere else.

The night before the graduation ceremonies, Mom and I knew there'd be trouble when Dad didn't come home. He didn't stay away overnight all that often, but when he did we knew he'd fallen into a poker game, probably at someone's farm, or a heavy drinking party that didn't know how to end. "It's always when something important is happening that he acts like this," my mom said. The last big public event in the family had been my brother's wedding two years before. The three of us had caught the night train from Swift Current to Winnipeg, where my brother was stationed in the Air Force, Dad with a bottle in his suit jacket, shouting and singing, keeping everyone awake until the porter threatened to throw him off. Shame was a large part of living with him, but that was the first time I willed myself to grow small, so small that no one could see me. Later I was startled when I caught the reflection of my face in the window of the train. I thought I had made myself disappear.

The afternoon of my graduation, my mom made me walk to the school to tell Mr. Whiteman, the teacher in charge, that my father wouldn't be at the banquet. He'd been called out of town for work, I was to say. The story was implausible because my father's job was in the oil fields, just a few miles away. I prayed that Mr. Whiteman didn't know what Dad did for a living, and I squirmed at the thought of lying to him. He was my English teacher, I'd just gotten 97 per cent on my Easter exam, and I wanted to keep his respect. Mr. Whiteman nodded his head and said nothing, but I saw something in his gaze that I'd never seen before. It wasn't disappointment or anger. Would I have known then to call it pity? Whatever it was, it made me mad, not at my parents or myself, but at him. The love I felt for my father was fierce and atavistic. It would have been easier if I could have simply hated him.

Now, a few hours later, I walk ahead of my parents to the school to relay the good news that my father is able to make it after all. The head table will need to be rearranged, my father's place card set beside mine. Trying to get to the gym before the other grads and their parents are seated, I walk as fast as I can, pounding my new thin heels so hard on the sidewalk that the rubber tip breaks off my right shoe. Mr. Whiteman is standing by the stage I helped decorate the day before with crepe paper streamers, Kleenex roses and balloons. When I move between the long tables across the floor toward him, one shoe makes a clicking noise; the other lands without a sound. I wish anything would happen but what's about to. I wish I were any other place on earth.

⁐

In his book *The Marriage of Cadmus and Harmony*, the Italian novelist Roberto Calasso distinguishes between two kinds of people: weavers and Dionysians. He explains that Dionysus "is not a useful god who helps weave or knot things together, but a god who loosens and unties. The weavers are his enemies. Yet there comes a moment when the weavers will abandon their looms to dash off after him into the mountains.

Dionysus is the river we hear flowing by in the distance, an incessant booming from far away." I was in my mid-twenties when I first heard that distant sound.

After high-school graduation, I went on to the University of Saskatchewan, in Saskatoon. In the middle of a four-year degree, I got married. My husband and I taught in a village in the north of the province for two years, then ended up back in my hometown, where I became an English teacher and guidance counsellor and he taught science. I was hard-working and responsible. My husband, a nondrinker, was as different from my father as he could possibly be. We lived on an acreage five miles south of town; we visited his parents in Regina every long weekend; we canoed, hiked, jogged, and went camping every summer with our dog. Life seemed conventional, predictable and safe. Then I discovered poetry.

At a summer school of the arts, where I went to work on my first manuscript, I met a group of writers I felt instantly at home with, and my shadow life began. We wrote poems, we drank, we danced, and a few of us had affairs during those three weeks spent away from husbands and wives. Many of us went back year after year. At the end of the session each summer, I'd return to my sober weaver's existence, threading together my marriage, my job, my in-laws. I began to think of starting a family, but I could hear that Dionysian river thrumming in my blood. I didn't know then it would soon drown out every other sound.

One day, Roberto Calasso says, the river "rises and floods everything, as if the normal above-water state of things, the

sober delimitation of our existence, were but a brief paren-
thesis overwhelmed in an instant." I met Patrick, and the
banks flooded. With barely a second thought, I pushed off
from the shores of my previous life, left my husband and
career for a stormy journey of lovemaking, fights, revelries
and poems. We thirsted for intensity; we savoured crises. And
right from the start, our passion for poetry and for each other
included drinking. We had what fancier people would have
called a cocktail late in the afternoon, wine over dinner, and
sometimes a brandy nightcap before we went to bed. On the
weekends we got sloshed and partied with friends. For our
first ten years, the drinking didn't get out of hand. At least,
neither of us saw it that way.

My mother has always been a weaver or, more accurately, a
knitter. She likes to plant her two feet firmly on familiar
ground, and she finds the taste of liquor in any form revolt-
ing. All the years when Dad stumbled home "drunker than a
skunk," as she would say, she never touched a drop. The first
Christmas after my father died, Patrick and I splurged on a
bottle of Dom Pérignon. We poured glasses for her, my
brother, his wife and ourselves, then proposed a toast. Before
we could click our glasses, Mom took a sip, ducked into the
kitchen, then reappeared beside us. When she raised her
champagne again, we noticed it was dark. "It's too sour," she
said. "I added some Coke."

Besides the few bottles of beer my father kept in the

garage or in the basement cold room where the garden potatoes were stored for the winter, there wasn't any booze in our
house. Dad did his drinking at the Legion, though he hadn't
been a soldier in any war; at the Eagles' Lounge, which was
open Sunday afternoons; and at the three hotel bars on Central Avenue: the Healy, the Imperial and the York. He'd get
home from work, wash his face and hands, change into a shirt
and tie, and leave for a few drinks before the bars closed
between five and seven. He'd return to the house to eat the
supper my mother had kept warm on the back of the stove,
then head out again until last call. I remember how upset she
was when the provincial liquor regulations changed and the
bars stopped closing over the supper hour. Home from university for the holidays, I argued for human liberty, freedom
of choice. "You don't understand," she said. "Now he won't
even take the time to eat."

It wasn't that she was particularly concerned about his
health. But without a good supper after working all day in the
oil patch, where would he find the strength to get up at 6 A.M.
and spend another eight hours at heavy labour? Food in his
stomach would keep his blood-alcohol level down, too. Twice
in three years he'd lost his driver's licence, a penalty that
meant one of his fellow workers had to pick him up in the
morning and drop him off at the end of their shift. Both times
the judge had allowed him dispensation to drive a backhoe in
the oil fields. Otherwise he would have lost his job.

My father didn't lie about his drinking. What would have

been the point? But never did I hear either of them use the word *alcoholic*. He drank, but he claimed he could hold his liquor. That ability was part of being a man, as was his right to spend his paycheque on anything he wanted. As was his prowess at arm-wrestling, shuffleboard and pool. The windowsills in our living room shone with trophies he'd brought home from the bars. They competed for space with the curling trophies he and Mom had won as skips of their own teams, though that game's prizes were often more practical—matching table lamps, a big wine-coloured ottoman made out of Naugahyde, a set of cutlery, a side of beef.

For Mom, his excess wasn't a disease; it stemmed from selfishness and a lack of affection for us. "He cares more about the Legion," she'd say. "He'd rather be with a bunch of drunks than his family." If he wasn't an alcoholic, if he could stop whenever he wanted to, the deficiencies were in us, not him. I wasn't good enough or pretty enough or smart enough to keep him home. Nor was she. He seemed to be having a good time, at least until he had to face her anger every morning before he left for work. She and I were the ones full of shame and anxiety and despair. We were the ones sitting at home each night, dreading his arrival, hoping we'd be in bed and could pretend to be asleep when he stumbled in the door.

Patrick called himself an alcoholic long before I was ready to hear it. I thought he was exaggerating. When I began to accept that he might be right, I admired his honesty, though the word *alcoholic*, like *cancer*, scared me. He needed to cut back, but what would it mean if he stopped altogether? Would I have to stop too? I didn't want to. After all, in our days of drinking, we'd had glorious times together. We'd written books; we'd received grants, awards and teaching jobs; and we'd been able to keep the vitality in our long relationship. We'd also done weavers' things: spent blissful days in the garden, renovated three old houses as we moved from place to place, built ponds, rescued and fallen in love with cats, and made extravagant dinners for our friends. Our lives were filled with shared passions, but also with moments of comfortable and deep companionship. At the same time, I'd recently found myself sinking into small pockets of despair.

Years before, I'd made some changes in my own drinking. I'd woken on a Sunday morning to one too many hangovers, one too many foggy memories of sloppy, embarrassing behaviour, Patrick's or mine. I began to question the equation we'd constructed when we first got together: one wild drinker + another = poetry and passion. I continued to delight in a glass or two of cool Chardonnay on my lips, but I'd cut back and, to my relief, the poetry and the passion had survived. There were still nights when I drank too much, but unlike Patrick, I could stop before the bottle was empty.

It's odd how living with obsessive drinking can feel fine one day and impossible the next. You wake up one morning and overnight someone has built a wall between you and that other life. Shouts and snatches of songs and conversations drift over the top, but though you long to join in, the gate that has always let you through remains firmly shut. I began to count how many glasses Patrick emptied compared to mine, how many times he dominated the conversation at a dinner party, how many evenings I had to drive us home. My tallies made me miserable.

Although Patrick had named his problem, he wasn't ready to do anything about it. I started to go to Al Anon, crying my way through the first meeting as if the years of sadness over my father's drinking, and now Patrick's, had funnelled into one narrow hour in a room full of strangers. At first I hoped my example would make Patrick see the light. How could he not at least control his drinking when he saw me heading out with such determination every Wednesday evening, a small book of daily meditations called *Courage to Change* in my hand? Didn't he love me enough to make me happy?

It didn't take many meetings for me to realize that he wasn't the only one with a problem. The eight or so people who sat around the table told stories similar to mine about searching for hidden bottles, about springing a son or daughter from jail, about lying to bosses and friends to cover up a spouse's misdemeanours, about doing everything imaginable to get the drinking to stop. Those who'd been going to meetings for a long time laughed uproariously at *their* bad behaviour. They laughed at how desperate and needy *they* had been. They even cracked jokes about living with booze:

"How do you know when an alcoholic's lying?" "When he moves his lips."

A year after my first meeting, Patrick went to AA with a friend who'd been dry for eight months. When he came home, he declared his drinking days were over. We agreed there'd be no booze in the house except a bottle of wine, so I could have my usual glass before dinner. That didn't bother him. It was the high-octane stuff he craved, he said. Although I'd lose my favourite drinking partner, my own habits wouldn't have to change that much; everything was going to be okay. I was jubilant, but then the lying began. Patrick hid bottles around the house where he thought I wouldn't see them, drank when I was at work, and switched to vodka because it didn't smell as strong on his breath as Scotch or brandy. "Are you okay?" I'd ask. "Yes," he'd say. "Just tired."

Living with lies is crazy-making. Your perceptions tell you one thing; the person you love most in the world tells you another. Are you insane? Have you turned into a paranoid fishwife? How pathetic are you? Metaphorically, sometimes literally, you get down on your knees. You say things like "Please, tell me the truth, I beg you" and "Tell me anything, I won't be angry, just don't lie." It's bad for both of you, it's bad for the relationship, it's an erosion of trust, you tell him. How would he feel if the shoe were on the other foot, you ask, if the bottle were in the other hand? He doesn't pause, doesn't blink. He looks you straight in the eye and says, "I'm not drinking." You want to believe him, but when he's behind the wheel he swings from the yellow line to the shoulder, he asks you the same question three times, he doesn't remember the name of the movie you're going to. "Have you been drinking?" Of course he has. The real question is why in the world it is so important for me to get him to admit it.

⌒

My mother always said "There's no better man than your father when he's sober." That comment made me furious as a kid. When was he sober? Why did she put up with it? I'm glad I had the sense not to push her for an answer. Limited by my judgemental child's eye, I had no idea of the private moments my parents shared. The afternoon she and my brother and I scattered Dad's ashes over the alkali lake on the farm where she grew up, she said "You made my life better" as the last of him drifted across the water. *Better?* Nothing could have shocked me more.

When I was fourteen, my mother got a job selling tickets at the Junior A Bronco hockey games. The rink was on the outskirts of town, a couple of miles from our house. She didn't have a driver's licence and couldn't rely on my dad to show up sober or on time, so she walked all winter through the dark and cold to the evening games. She did this for more than twenty years, until she was well into her seventies. Sometimes she'd get a ride home with a fellow worker; if not, she'd make the trek back again. I can still see her small bundled figure trudging through the snow, the icy wind whipping around her. When I call up the memory, it's as if I'm watching her from high above and she's the only moving thing in all that white.

She and I set off on several similar walks together when I was little. Once, after we'd waited for an hour for Dad to pick us up from the Eagles' Christmas party, a brown bag of hard, striped candy clutched in my hand, we headed out down the dark and snowy streets alone. Mom had refused offers of other rides. The temperature had fallen to thirty below, and she couldn't believe he wouldn't come. Halfway home, because I was shivering, she undid the big buttons on her old muskrat coat and pulled me inside, the back of my head pressing into her belly, the satin lining slipping across my forehead and nose. What strange tracks we must have printed in the snow as I blindly shuffled my feet between hers. It was an intimacy I revelled in, a return to the warmth, smell and darkness of my mother's body. Can I see it now as a gift my father gave me? Or am I struggling too hard to find forgiveness?

Sunday afternoons my father spent drinking in the Eagles' Lounge. When it closed, he came home with a Fat Emma or Pie Face chocolate bar for Mom and me, and after supper we'd eat them watching *The Ed Sullivan Show* on our first television set, a big wooden Fleetwood in the centre of the living room. A scrawny eight-year-old, I'd sit by Dad on the couch, as close as I could get, to play what he called "wrestling" and I secretly called "the hand-hurting game." I'd bend back his thumbs until he cried uncle. I'd push the flesh of his fingertips over his closely bitten nails. This would go on for the whole hour, me trying to hurt my father. I delighted in our physical closeness, and he seemed to like my needy aggression, telling me how strong I was and pretending to be in pain. At the time I thought his cries of injury were real. I was always the one who initiated the game, and he patiently let me maul his fingers until I decided to stop.

Only now, more than forty years later, have I figured out what this all-consuming game meant to me. I loved my father's hands. Big-knuckled, strong from manual labour, they were often scraped and oil-stained. Harming them became my way of touching him and of having him touch me. It was our only body contact. I hurt him into loving me.

I don't damage Patrick physically, for pretend or for real. But I wound him in other ways. I know he suffers when he sees how wrecked his drinking makes me. Am I really *that* injured? Or do I play a martyr role, wet-eyed and helpless, to see his pain? How much of my adult life is darkened by my father's long shadow? When does the woman I've become fall away and that kid, with all her fear, hurt and anger festering just beneath the surface, take my place?

☞

Patrick is a person I can depend upon. When he says he'll be home at a certain time or promises to meet me with the car, he always shows up. Unlike my mother, I've never been that lone figure cutting through the cold while a man who has forgotten me racks the pool balls and knocks back another beer. But in my head, over and over, I've walked my mother's walk. Alcoholism—whether you're the drinker, the child, the husband or the wife—places you in a winter landscape. It takes you far beyond the warmly lit windows where other families gather around a table laden with their evening meal. It numbs you, it orphans you, it widows.

Alistair MacLeod's novel *No Great Mischief* opens with a family's disappearance beneath Atlantic ice. The narrator describes a small space between the water and the ice where you can open your mouth and breathe. As I read, I can't stop myself from seeing it as the place that drinking takes you. It's as if the Dionysian waters, without any warning, have frozen over. There are days when my own breathing space feels that constricted, that small. When I try to disappear in the train, when I lie to my favourite teacher, when I look for bottles in the back yard in the middle of the night, I'm there. And when I ask for the hundredth time "Have you been drinking?" my legs, treading water as hard as they can, barely keep my mouth above the surface.

When you're trapped between those two worlds, Mac-Leod's narrator says, taking your last sips of air before your body succumbs to the cold, you must look for a change in the light along the underbelly of the ice to see where you fell through. Then, while there's time—and there are only minutes—you must kick to the hole and hoist yourself up. That's what you have to do in spite of the draw of the long darkness

below. I need to find the broken spot where Patrick and I
went under. I hope we can get there together. Spreading our
weight evenly across the ice, we will pull ourselves, hand by
hand, word by word, over the wide expanse of cold and onto
the rocky shore.

The excerpt from The Marriage of Cadmus and Harmony *by
Roberto Calasso is translated by Tim Parks and quoted by him in
"Adultery," an essay in his book* Adultery and Other Diversions
(New York: Arcade Publishing, 1998).

Drinking

David Adams Richards

When I was four my grandfather, who'd been drunk for days, bought my sister a horse—a bowled, wobbly draft he brought to the front of our bungalow. We were at the door watching as my mother went out to meet him. She was pregnant again, and an outsider among her in-laws; an outsider in our town of Newcastle, in which we as a family were also in a certain way outsiders.

Though we were willing to care for it—house it in the garage, feed it beets—my mother broke our hearts by telling him we couldn't accept it. This was quite an insult in front of the men he drank with, who had talked him into buying it. So he cursed her in front of those men.

We did not get the horse. Nor did we know we were part of a power play Grampie had concocted, silly little dupes for the grown-up world. My mother putting her foot down on the edge of our dry lot quashed the grandeur he had tried to obtain by spending my grandmother's money.

My grandfather came to our house at breakfast the next day to continue his tirade, and my father, with shaving cream still covering half his face, came out of the bathroom and told him to leave. There was shoving at the door, but my father, though uniformly a pacifist, was as strong as a bull. So my grandfather left, hat and suit askew, railing abuse at us all.

My father didn't drink, for he had seen what it had done to his stepfather—our Grampie. I could see my father shaking as he came inside, in anger and bewilderment. Bewilderment for his uncles, who were numbered among the town drunks. They were men of my blood.

When I was little, drink surrounded me as rivers did fish. It lay in the burdocks and pissed its pants, or came at me zigzagging up walkways, answering to the names of forgotten cousins and family members gone off to Boston years before. It acquired taste and wore suits and carried on its person, in 1956, golden folded pocket-watch chains, or carried hand purses, and fashionable gloves, down to our one good restaurant on some forgotten May afternoon to order sandwich slices and rye whisky. It listened to elevator music in the offices of the movie theatre that my family owned, and could recite psalms and talk about St. Augustine. It had a yearning for sophistication never quite achieved, and ached on rainy days in the back rooms of small houses. It blossomed at weddings, got sentimental at baptisms; it carried the weight of a sagged paunch, had a sad grin or light whimsical eyes at forty.

It trotted out bad poetry at St. Patrick's Day concerts and railed against the English all over again. And again. And again.

So before I ever drank or sang an Irish rebel song or shouted out in joy and rebellion, drink was part of me. And not only was there drinking in our family: we employed drinkers as well, at our theatre. The ones I admired were dutiful-minded; there was something great about their affliction—drawn to our theatre and each other, they had the mark of genuine humanity. They watched Bogie thwack the bad guys, drive a boat blind in fog, grin through his whisky and cigarette smoke.

Back in the fifies, when these men were in their twenties, they ran projection machines and took tickets, chewed peppermints to mask the smell of wine, stood waiting for drives home at dark in freezing weather without hat or mitts, more like Bogie than they would ever know. Sooner or later they drifted off or moved away.

Drink surrounded me, coaxed me gently with its timeless serenade, told me that it would wait, bide its time, and be there whenever I turned to embrace it.

When I was eight years of age my family moved to a section of town called "the Rocks" that overlooked the crystal Miramichi River. It was a harsher and wilder part of town, with families not only blue-collar but desperately poor. Here, on May nights filled with the whiff of snow, prostitutes as young as sixteen would wait for strange foreign sailors, accepting in payment foreign utterances of devotion and a bottle of wine. I passed them lying down on cardboard boxes in the flare of fires as I walked up the small pathway with my little sister. We saw men sitting out on the banks to drink who had, like my great uncles, been shot up in the first war or gassed at Ypres. I knew them by name, and was conscious of a certain decayed splendour they had.

By twelve I began to hear my name called by those who mocked what they considered in error my father's money and my lame left side, lame because of a fall my mother had when she was seven months pregnant with me. Because of this I was always something of an outcast. I understood that I was different and I suppose I was alone.

All of this was diligent recruitment for the bottle. Yet as a boy I could never picture myself with a drink in my hand. The only thing my father ever requested of me, on one of our trips to Saint John, was for me not to drink. Still I knew it was near me. Sometimes it came into the house with the cold, off the breath of some playful uncle, and slapped me on the knee and laughed. Or it coursed through the veins of certain bleary-eyed men my father did business with in Saint John. (I accompanied him only so I could go to a restaurant and have an elevator ride.)

At first on occasion, and then on a more regular basis, I began to see drink in youngsters I knew. They drank in caves or shacks overlooking the river, their faces drenched white by their breath or the light from weak light bulbs. I knew that soon something would be required of me.

The first two people my age I saw drunk were the son of a judge and a boy that judge had put in jail. They offered me

beer. I shook my head no. They mocked me. I went home.
Yet, thinking of the reputation it carried within my family, I
promised myself I would never drink. I made that promise in
October of 1964. I began to drink that December, at the time
I began to read books. I was given a beer on Christmas Eve.
Flushed with lights and joyous celebration, all seemed possi-
ble. I was also given a copy of *Oliver Twist* that same Christ-
mas, and my love of books and writing was born.

By fifteen I was drinking now and again, a bottle of beer
or a quart of wine. Sometimes I bought it myself, staring at
the bottle as a foreigner. Often the beer tasted like potato
peelings, or the wine was too sweet. We drank in groups on
special occasions. After a time there was no need for special
occasions—whenever we managed to find something to
drink, well, that was special enough.

Looking back now, I see I drank with many kids whose
families had histories of drink. We were establishing ourselves as the next generation. From the first I didn't drink
naturally—but neither did any of my friends. We came from
a hard-drinking river, though, and after a certain period we
all drank heavily, continuing until we quit or were killed or
found ourselves chronic alcoholics.

I was discernibly different from most of my friends in one
way. I literally *loved* to drink alone. If I was still drinking, I
still would.

The town library had three floors, and on the top floor
was a locked room. It was the French room, with French
books, and a friend of mine had obtained a key. No one else

ventured up there, and with the door locked it made a comfortable place to while away the afternoons when I was
thought to be in school. I had no use for school, but, as I
mentioned, I loved books. And many of these French texts
had side-by-side English translations. So I drank wine and
read François Villon in the old nineteenth-century manse.
When the librarian locked the front door and left for home,
I would venture into the rooms downstairs and read until well
after dark. I also started to write my own sketches there.

As my drinking and skipping school became more fre-
quent, I became more of a problem. I rebelled in a violent,
almost anarchistic way. I came to class late or snuck in a bottle
with me. Since I was small compared to others, I would fight
at the least provocation. Finally I was suspended, then expelled.
I was told the only way I'd be allowed back in school would
be if I saw a psychiatrist and took the strap. I was in a funny
position, forced to see a psychiatrist and take the strap in
order to be allowed access to someplace I never wanted to be.

However, I did graduate and was accepted by St. Thomas
University. Here I drank more, and partied harder. It was
here that a friend took me aside and cautioned me one afternoon. If I was invited to his parents' house he wanted me
sober. It was the first time anyone had ever said anything to
me about my drinking, and it provoked me. I did not go to his
house or visit him again.

During these years a number of friends and acquain-
tances I had grown up with were killed. Most of them died, in

one way or another, because of drink. I wanted to write about all of this, and I started a novel.

But my writing seemed very much like everything else in my life. No one thought me much good. So I quit university and went to Europe. There I drank every day. I got drunk only once, but I came back home with an appreciation for the morning drink.

At twenty-one I got married to the girl who had stood beside me during my high-school visits to the psychiatrist. We lived at first in a room in Fredericton, with a hot plate and a single cot. The bathroom was two flights up. We got our own little apartment on King Street some months later, and it was there I wrote what would become my first published novel, *The Coming of Winter*. After that was done, we moved to another apartment, on Saint John Street, where I started my second novel, *Blood Ties*.

I was twenty-three, twenty-four years old. I was drinking almost every day and taking downers (which I thought were a great complement to a drink, and had gotten from the second psychiatrist I was asked to see). By now I was aware that I could not stop drinking. This was fine, because I did not want to stop. But it did cause problems. I was a far heavier drinker than most of my friends from university, and certain of them began to shun me. My wife, Peggy, left on two or three occasions. Each time I would straighten out and tell myself, and her, that I would stop drinking.

After *Blood Ties* was finished, Peggy and I left for Europe.

I felt alienated among the other Canadian artists and writers I met there. I was not the kind of liberal that was in vogue in the seventies; my work seemed to be in direct opposition to the communal spirit of the time, which I felt was bogus. Drink protected me from these ideals I could not take seriously, while hiding my belief in a kind of individual anarchism. I could hide in the bottle, and there was always another bottle after that. Drink let me pretend to be like others while the whole course of my life cried out for me to be something else.

Back in Canada, Peggy decided we must do something about my drinking. So we tried the geographical cure. She picked a spot on the map and we went there, literally to the other side of Canada—Victoria.

We rented an apartment, bought a card table from the Salvation Army. I set up my typewriter and went out for a walk. This was the first of many "walks" in which I would disappear from home, sometimes for days—drinking. Every time I told myself that I would have only one drink. But of course that never happened. The first drink led to more and more. I would start for home but never make it. After I'd been on an almost continuous seven-month drunk, we headed back to New Brunswick. I had completed one story in all that time. I believed I was washed up as a writer, and many of my writing friends were available to tell me this was so—because if you make your name young, like Billy the Kid, there is a price on your head.

It would take well over three years to write my next book,

Lives of Short Duration. During this time Peggy and I moved again, to the worst place possible for me—our hometown.

The blackouts became regular. Each time I drank there would be hours, even days I could not remember. I would start to work and manage to get three pages done. Then, thinking three pages was a wonderful amount, I would go to the bookshelf where I kept my bottle of rum and have one drink, then two. I would leave the house before Peggy got home from work. The night stretched out before me, and many times the next day.

We went back to Europe. For a while Peggy tried to keep up with my drinking. She would sit with me sometimes, and we'd drink through the night. But one night would never do it for me. So Peggy would go to bed, and I would find myself at the bar at nine in the morning drinking beer. Of course, beer was nothing more than piss, so I would drink a few and then buy rum.

I decided that a three-day drunk was nothing to be ashamed of. After all, I was a writer—and all the writers whose work I cared for drank. All the writers I *knew* drank, in fact, and I was younger than most of them by ten or twenty years.

At a point in my life when I had begun to drink alone in earnest, Peggy provided me with the twenty questions. Answer three in the affirmative and you are an alcoholic, she said. I checked yes to nineteen out of twenty. The only one I did not answer yes to was "Does alcohol cause problems between you and fellow workers?" Of course not. I had no fellow workers.

Yet now, when I really wanted to stop, when I prayed to be able to drink normally, I could not. Nor could I control anything I did or said once I started drinking. It was a terrible feeling, not to know what was to happen to me once I went outside. Three-day drunks became three-week drunks, and then three-month drunks.

I would return to my wife and my study in tremors, filled with remorse. I would look at my manuscript in progress and realize I hadn't put a word to paper in weeks. I would, as my sister-in-law once told me, literally stink of booze. I would remember snatches and snippets of conversation, realizing that I had been somewhere, had spoken about something. The words would come at me, pierce my skin like bullets. I would remember railing and ranting at someone—perhaps a friend—and then I would hear that I had threatened someone, or someone had threatened me.

I would vow not to drink again.

I lay on the couch, holding a Bible in my hand (I'm still not sure why), and drifted in and out of horrors. I almost always saw dragonflies flying about the room. I would hear my name being called, and I would sit up, sweat pouring off me, waiting for an intruder who never came.

After a few days, with some proper food and rest, the shaking and the itching would go away. The demons would recede. I would go back to work for a day or two. Then, seeing my chance (an argument with Peg or something else), I would go downtown once more, sure that I would only have a drink or two and be home in time for supper.

But from the time I was twenty-three, a drink or two never happened. Worse for me was the fact that certain people believed I wrote terrible things about the Miramichi. The idea many had was that I sent Peg out to work so I could drink and write "dirty books." They were right about one thing—I had earned no money in years.

I had descended pretty much into hell. It took a long while to get out, for a writer is a strange beast, and so many of my plans revolved around drinking. Drinking is good for the creative mind, I told myself. Drinking liberates you from the mundane and the pedestrian. Drinking is a brilliant man's weakness. Those who don't drink are uninspired, callow cogs. Better dead than becoming one of those artificial, church-going, gossip-slinging mannequins.

One by one those vague absolutes had to disappear. But they were hard to get rid of. I wrecked our car and did not rid myself of them. I was thrown in jail and they did not loosen their hold upon me. My friends turned away from me. Still my central idea of drink as romantic and inspirational continued.

My greatest fear of all, of course, was failure. I could do nothing else in life but write. How, then, could I face up to failure as a writer? Bad enough to face up to being a failure as a husband or a human being. But as a writer, like poor Scott Fitzgerald, you could still be called a *brilliant* failure. If I chose to quit drinking, I would have no crutch to fall back on when I failed. And by the time I was thirty, everything pointed to my failure.

That idea, compounded by the feeling that my drinking friends were the wisest and most brilliant people I knew, put me in a Catch-22. If I quit, what would they say about me? Did I want them to talk about me as a teetotaller? Never. For what had I said about teetotallers myself? Yet weeks would go by and no friend would call. And in my house, bottles were hidden for those occasions when the demons visited.

The December I was thirty-one, swollen up to 189 pounds, I borrowed a thousand dollars from the bank for presents. I did not buy one present. I bought cocaine and rum and beer, and I started to drink and snort coke midway through the month. Christmas had never been a particularly joyous occasion for me. Worse, my new book, *Lives of Short Duration*, had arrived, and I hated the cover. I was frightened of the pending reviews. I was also bothered by the fact that Peg had bought us skis that year. How could I ski with a bad leg? I couldn't. What would people say when they saw me trying? Better to get drunk and stoned and forget it. Or to go skiing drunk and high on coke. I could always write about it later.

Peggy celebrated Christmas alone, went to midnight mass by herself.

On Boxing Day, my rum and cocaine gone, I sat at the kitchen table with a case of beer, nursing a hangover. Everything in our house seemed desolate. Then Trapper, a friend I had not seen in months, came to the door. He sat on one side of the table, Peg on the other. I sat in the middle, piling beer into myself, looking at both of them.

I had never thought of AA. And when Trapper started speaking to me about it, I had exactly the same feeling that many others have had—what in hell does this guy know about life compared to me?

The thing was, he didn't say he knew more about life than me. He just said: "You're using booze to fight booze— you hit the bottle, it will always hit you back."

Then he said he had been sober for three months. Three months was an eternity. I looked at him and almost laughed. I didn't believe him.

"How in hell did you stay sober for three months?"

"Just come to a meeting," he said.

"You want me to go to a meeting?" I asked Peg.

"I think you should," she answered.

That too was surprising. I had thought she would say, no, you're not that bad yet.

So I told him I would go—but that I wanted to go there the back way. There must be a route we could take where no one would see me? But what was worse, the meeting was that night. He told me he would come and get me at a quarter to eight.

It all seemed too much too soon. For the rest of the day I tried to find some way out. I blamed Peg for getting me into it. But that day I could not get sober and I could not get drunk. I was stuck in no man's land. At quarter to eight Trapper arrived, and I angrily left the house with him.

I had passed the building we arrived at two thousand times without knowing it was an AA hall. But from the first words of the first speaker at my first meeting, I realized that someone else had felt all the things I had, and had done most of them himself; and I felt at home.

I went to AA every second day. I did not drink for one whole month—the longest I had been sober since I was fifteen. Then I went to Ontario on a reading tour. In Ottawa I decided to have a glass of wine. Peggy asked me not to. Don't be ridiculous, I told her. I had not had a drink in a month, and one drink would not hurt. I picked up the wine. I looked at it. I closed my eyes as I drank it. It was seven o'clock on January 26. I would not draw a sober breath until April.

As before, the demons came back. But for some terrible reason, now they were ten times worse—just as the people at AA had told me they would be. Feeling there was no hope, I decided I would drink until I died. I went for drives dead drunk, closing my eyes for snatches of sleep while doing sixty miles an hour. I would wake up in strange places, drive a hundred miles for a drink at a bar where no one knew me. The drunk went on and on and on. It was a deadly drunk in which I tried to kill myself and threatened to kill others. I snuck about town at night, kept myself hidden all day. I drank and did coke with abandon. Finally I found myself at the hospital door, dropped off by someone I had been drinking with.

When they started to admit me, I, ashamed and scared, balked and went home.

The house was empty. It was desolate as always. We had not bought a new piece of furniture in years, because I drank up almost everything. Peggy was at work, and the humming of the fridge almost drove me catatonic. So I telephoned Trapper. Once again he came, 220 pounds of muscle and a sweet smile on his face. I remembered how he and I and another friend had gone on weeklong benders, how we had arrived in the Gaspé in a hearse, and how I had thrown a knife though the foot of our drinking buddy. I remembered how Trapper, on a binge, had taken a taxi to Newfoundland, how he had knocked a man cold for a drink of wine. He had once been one of the toughest men on the river. That night he sat down and watched me as I paced the floor. I couldn't sleep, couldn't eat, couldn't do anything but shiver, hot and cold, seeing shadowy figures and hearing my name called. The horrors went on and on. I looked and felt like a man on the way to the gallows.

"Think you'd like to go to a meeting?" he said.

I went back to AA. It was April 2, 1982. I thought people would feel superior to me. But when I walked in, people smiled at me and shook my hand. I hung around. But it wasn't easy. It wasn't easy at all. Sometimes it still isn't. It took months before I felt human, and three years before I was able to complete another book. But since then I have written ten more. Since then, by luck and by God, and though I have been sorely tempted, I have never taken another drink.

Blackout

Sheri-D Wilson

Narcotics cannot still the tooth,
that nibbles at the soul.

—EMILY DICKINSON

With a final gesture of good-bye, and my ten-speed tightly secured to the roof of my old Olds, I ran off in 1982 to join the circus maximus poeticus. Among language contortionists and red-nosed clowns, my high-flying aerial act would become legendary from town to town as the Sheri-D Show.

I suppose the whole notion of the Sheri-D Show was conceived on an airplane from Toronto back to my home-town of Calgary when I was seventeen. An older gentleman sat in the seat next to mine. He asked me what I did. I told him I was a poet, and I asked him what he did. He told me *he* was a poet. Sure, buddy, I thought. Don't you know that poets don't really exist? And if they did they wouldn't be on a flight to Calgary? Aren't you a little old to be making up im-pressive dream professions on airplanes? Turns out he really was a poet, though, a well-known one. At that age, all I could do was dream, in my imaginary circus tights, that somehow my lie, my fantasy, my imaginary me would one day come into being.

I wasn't going to be the goody-goody bunhead from Calgary, Alberta, who married, had kids, and dreamed of all the things she might have seen and done. Oh no. I was going to go out into the world and do something different. I would be the outspoken girl who said and did everything. I would be the one who smoked and drank and swore and did drugs and had wild sex and wrote poetry and made jazz till dawn like the women I had read about. My behaviour would not be limited by my gender. Somehow, I was going to reinvent myself from a sweet, starry-eyed, working-class small-town innocent into an irreverent, well-travelled, well-read, exotic, free-spirited jazz poet. I'd be the dame who'd outdo any man. Drink them under the table in a rally of hilarity, vulgarity and intellect of light-speed and bullwhip slash. The only question was how.

My transition from bunhead to bard began when a friend suggested I attend acting school. Since I had no money, university entrance or other modus operandi, that is what I did. At acting school, the excitement of literature entered the skeleton of my being, making me vibrate with tintinnabulations of euphoric discovery. It was as if all the acting students were coming to life together, and the world stood before us like a big ripe Bing cherry. I would attend classes dressed as Mata Hari or Patti Smith or Virginia Woolf and deliver long diatribes of invented bravado.

One Saturday night I walked across the 10th Street bridge en route to Ten Foot Henry's, the hip hot spot for Calgary's late-seventies alternative art crowd, with the elongated stride of my nineteen years. The Mistress of Wintriness snapped her subzero fingers and the river steamed in hoarer on the verge of shape-shifting into a standstill. My feet moved in sync with my impatience to party, almost percolating a permafreeze tap dance along the glass-glaze runner of the sidewalk. When the secret door to Henry's opened, a blast of warm air and loud music came cascading out onto the street, sweet as a long swoon. I paid my cover, and I was off to the rampage. Postdisco inferno on a Dionysian night. Nothing could stop my strut. I drank shooters from my body flask for the feeling of contraband inebriation. Smoked Cheech and Chong spliff, and snorted lines as long as Molly Bloom's soliloquy from oversized purse mirrors in toilet stalls. Bodies snaked sensual as a belly dancer's undulation around the curves of beatitude, free love, passionate poetry and R&B loud enough to boom through my bones like a Goliath timpani. There were madcap projections of art on the walls, couches downstairs for the greenroom-cool and me and the band. Everyone seemed to have a flair for the unacceptable. This was the scene. I was in it—and I was out of it. Totally. I remember someone handing me a joint, and then there was . . . a *Cat on a Hot Tin Roof* click, and then there was . . . spinning, and then there was . . . nothing. I don't remember the river that took me home that night, but somehow that's where I ended up.

The next afternoon I was in the bathtub dreaming of the South Seas, looking deeply into the postcard of the Cook Islands taped, with curling corners, beside the four-legged tub. Every hue of tropical blue was trying to distract me from a metal-bending headache when my roommate knocked. "There's someone here for dinner."

"Okay, I'll be right out," I bellowed, before whooshing underwater. I didn't have any idea who was coming for dinner. Blub, blub, blub. I hadn't invited anyone. But the doorbell kept ringing and ringing. When I finally dressed and entered the living room there it was, an octopus with a bottle in each arm—eight men and eight bottles of wine. Not bad for a girl who couldn't get a date in high school. A scene from *Twenty Thousand Leagues under the Sea*, happening in my own living room. May the best sucker win, I remember thinking, may the best sucker win.

I squeezed myself out of the headlock/bottleneck by phoning a few girlfriends, ordering oodles of pizzas, and having a really good time. Later I heard a joke about being invited to my house for dinner. I felt like an urban myth. The first time I had pulled the roulette trigger of blackout obliteration, I had become a legend in my own time. Suddenly I was Dorothy Parker at the Algonquin, Charles Bukowski in female form. I had instantly become eccentric and mysterious, with a Patti Smith–like contempt for the dangerous. I'd dared to sample the bite-sized hors d'oeuvres of blowfish and lived to talk about it. The Sheri-D Show had premiered.

After acting school, I became interested in alternative approaches to the craft. I auditioned for a West Coast theatre that worked with the Odin technique, and I was hired as a company member. In Victoria I met people who took a vested interest in my education, and I realized the best way for me to learn was to find my own teachers/masters. Theatre was the perfect place for me to unravel writing through continual analysis of text and character. I was hungry for new perception, and I started writing my own texts. After my contract with the company expired, I moved to Vancouver, where I began performing my writings in galleries, living rooms and clubs: anywhere they'd listen to me. I met people from the same mind-tribe everywhere. After my first performance piece, *Tight Wire*, was performed in 1983, the Melmoth Group (West Coast surrealists) asked me to join them. It was a huge turning point in my educational process, like being given the gift of new eyes.

In the late eighties poetry entered my life for real. I was twenty-eight when I attended Naropa (the Jack Kerouac School of Disembodied Poetics) in Boulder, Colorado, as a noncredit student. The first night, I went to the opening dance, and before I knew it I was totally ripped. Everyone else split early because they wanted to meditate in the morning, but I was still on fire. I thought I was going to explode with excitement. On my way home I suddenly imagined I was in a musical. There I was, performing a beatnik song-and-dance number down the middle of the street, running and jumping and howling like Kerouac in *Dharma Bums*, flying through the air singing at the top of my lungs. And then, somewhere in the middle of the ecstatic air, I hit a streetlamp shadow and couldn't see the ground below. There was a split second when I felt everything go out of sync. And then I heard my ankle snap. I screamed blue murder, but there was no one around to hear my yowl as I dragged my poor foot home behind me, whimpering like an injured dog. The next day I went to the hospital and got the inescapable cast and crutches. I couldn't believe it. There I was at a Buddhist university with a broken ankle. Everyone gave me that someone's-telling-you-to-slow-down look. And I gave them my I-know-I-know-I've-got-a-lot-to-learn look back. But it amazes me how long it actually took me to see the connection between dying and death.

I will never forget the curse of triumph that rushed through my veins when Anne Waldman pronounced "You're a poet." I had been ordained by the Holy Mother of Poetry herself. It was happening. I was starting to live inside my own dreamscape. Studying, meditating, attending readings and lectures, and partying with my lifeline idols: ringmaster Anne Waldman, poetry high priestess Diane Di Prima, white clown Allen Ginsberg, torch-song juggler Peter Lamborn Wilson, cannon-blasted daredevil William S. Burroughs, set designer David Hockney, ring announcer Marianne Faithfull, and organ grinders Michael McClure and Ray Manzarek. I was the great trapezist Martini partying with the crème de la crème of the big top. This was the cirque de la scène for the party elite, and I was part of it. My dreams of aerial acrobatics were manifesting. I wanted to go higher, with no safety lines. I wanted to breathe fire, juggle chain saws, and tame wild tigers with whips and chairs. At the same time, it hit me on the head like an anvil that to become an artist would take a huge amount of work. For the first time I felt the weight of the slippers I had chosen to wear.

A few years later I was in Toronto at a massive early-winter theatre fund-raising booze-schmooze. Everyone was decked out in true eighties Toronto style, black leather jackets adorned with cock rings to look tough, with just enough colour to appear New York City–smooth. There was hair everywhere except on the skinheads. I was surrounded by gazillions of glamazons I hadn't seen for eons, and we were all in high form, having a blast, talking and dancing and flirting and laughing. We were the Warhol scene of our time, god-damn it. Someone gave me a strip of free drink tickets, and I was off.

I had just toured eastern Canada with Marianne Faithfull and Barry Reynolds, then checked out their concert/recording at St. Ann's Church in New York City, and I felt the cachet of my NYC swish as I regaled small groups of artists with stories of my latest exploits. The Sheri-D Show was in full swing. I'd learned that all a rapturous anecdote required was the resin of truth and a witty punchline. My life could sound as interesting as I wanted, and booze helped me exaggerate my trendy fairy tales to mythical proportions.

After a while I stepped outside and found the perfect spot

for fresh air and a cigarette under a wrought-iron fire escape. The booze was playing pick-up sticks with my head. Halfway through my smoke a wild-looking woman joined me. She didn't look like the other partiers; she was older, harder and closer to the streets. She had enough street smarts to devastate any New York City swarm, I thought to my drunken self, in her black matted fur, with her pointed rat-woman nose. She WAS theatre, the real thing, and the people inside were merely impersonators. I was already ripped, but when she reached her short, dirty fingers into her breast pocket and revealed a fatty with the revelation of a master magician, I couldn't say no. One drag and I felt the familiar Tennessee Williams click. I promised to go by her studio sometime . . . click . . . click . . . click . . . This rat could sniff out the darkest hiding spot in any sewer. She ruled the place where cats got lost and never returned. Top rat to Nosferatu. Queen of the Underground. She scared the living shit outta me. I took one last puff, and I was out of there. Poof.

Riding a rat-tail undertow back to the party, by now in full underwater swing. Breaking everyone moving in slow motion between strobes popping echos enlarged across synchronized sea floor lights bending into nautilus boomerangs coloured slur red mouths laugh in wide ruby scales eyes closed in blue eyeshadow Scotch another Scotch lights hit a sea of dancing leather infrared rat eyes laser through studs flicker. Suddenly everyone's leaving. Put on coat stand outside. Shiver follow rat-woman cram into cab

body-parts elbows backs of heads tails bending arrive
somewhere spill out of car. Air bites my skin with a cold-
blooded shark's tooth.

Inside there's a studio with all these bicycles hanging
upside down. Hundreds of bicycles rafters of bicycles
millions and millions of spokes a sky of wheels. Man Ray's
dream home. Fellini's. Loud music. Lines and lines and lines
on mirrors. I notice squid eyes staring. Who'd she come
with? I can hear them think. They all hate me. Smell a rat.
Time to make a break. Outside stars in snowlights. Lonely.
Somewhere. Walk. Walk. Door slightly ajar, go in, lie down,
close eyes.

I woke in the early morning, sick as a dog, lying on somebody's couch still dressed in my coat and boots and black
velvet hat. Whose house was I in? What city? No idea. No
sign of life. I tiptoed out. Around me the smells of Toronto's
Kensington Market opened, the bustle of bazaar stirred. I
hailed a cab and went back to the place where I was staying.
My friends served me packages of chicken noodle soup to
help my electrolytes as I pieced together a poem of the night.
"Pissed as a Sewer Rat," I called it.

I was becoming as addicted to the Sheri-D Show as I was
to the booze. Somehow the two went together. I was completely absorbed by the constant chaos, the shenanigans,
word quips, poetry and troublemaking that would unravel
around me when I drank. I was the social epicentre of hilarity,
my adventures side-splitting anecdotes I would later use in

my writing. Everyone seemed to love the half-cut Sheri-D. Back in Vancouver, I did poetry readings for a small fee and an unlimited bar tab. Wasn't that how poets were supposed to act? The way I saw it, the more I drank, the more money I was making. And the more calamity and danger I experienced, the more I desired, like going deeper and deeper into a subterranean city of the unknown. If my work was going to reflect my life, as my life reflected my work, everything had to be taken to the cutting edge. I didn't want to be seen as a fake, which meant I had to be the real thing. A sense of risk dominated every episode of the Sheri-D Show. It was reality TV before its time. My body could barely withstand the strain I was putting on it with one death-defying act after another. But luckily, I had a dancer's stamina and discipline. No matter how bad I felt, I never stopped doing my work.

The nineties came in with a bang. I had my first play professionally produced, my second book was published, and I was travelling extensively doing poetry readings and performance pieces. Life had never looked so good. I was back and forth between Lotusland and the Big Apple so much I felt like a flea in a windstorm.

When a close friend suggested I "be careful" with my drinking, I thought her ridiculous. How could I give up drinking? It was a crucial part of who I was. It had become part of my identity as an antimaterialist neo-beat poet. Sheri-D the drinker was invited everywhere, because people loved the madness that ensued. That Sheri-D was in big demand. What would she do next? Just wind her up with a few cocktails and watch her go crazy. And I *was* crazy, completely nuts, experiencing blackout after blackout.

I attended a poetry retreat in the mountains. Poets from all over North America had gathered to do readings and share ideas. The drinking began early and ended late. After a dance where we'd consumed enough alcohol to capsize a large oceangoing vessel, a poet friend invited me to come back to his room to smoke a joint and listen to music. We'd been chatting for about half an hour when there was a knock at the door. He yelled, "Just a minute." Then he turned to me and whispered, "As I was leaving the dance, a large woman asked if she could come back to my room and have sex."

"So?"

"That must be her."

"So?"

"Go into the bathroom and hide."

"That's stupid. I'll just leave."

"No. She can't know you've been here, 'cause then you'd know she'd been here."

For some strange reason this made sense to me, and the next thing I know I'm in a dark bathroom, pissed and stoned to the gills, with my ear pressed to the door. I hear him let her in, and then he returns to the bathroom, runs the tap, and gives me my next set of instructions. "Okay, I'm gonna go out there, and when we start doin' it, you tiptoe out of the room without her seeing you."

"Are you fucking crazy?"

"Please, just do it, for me, please."

"Okay, okay, okay. God!"

He turns off the tap, and once again I'm standing in a dark bathroom wondering how I got myself into this; better still, how I am going to get myself out. Within minutes I hear them getting it on. I opened the door a crack to peek, and I couldn't believe what I saw. My friend was completely buried under the largest naked woman I had ever seen. She was so enormous her body actually rippled over the sides of the single bed. I opened the door a little wider. She was riding him like a great white elephant on top of a mouse. I hoped he was still alive under there. I eased slowly out of the bathroom. As I slinked along the wall, I could see small pieces of him, reaching out from behind the flab, and he was making bold gestures pointing me in the direction of the door. I smiled at him in defiance and stood there watching in total disbelief. Then I tiptoed across the room, licked my fingers, and I stuck them up the fat girl's ass. Just like that. She jumped with excitement, turned her huge body slightly back, smiled, and continued riding the mouse-poet. Obviously I hadn't thought this one through! What do you do when you've got your fingers stuck up a fat girl's ass? Where do you go from there? What do you say? I slapped her vast white butt a few times and then I withdrew my phallus-fingers and I flew, out the door and down the hall. I was frantic. I couldn't believe what I had just done, but it made me laugh in wild bursts of madness. There was loud music and voices at the end of the hall, so I ran in that direction. Out of breath, feeling like a cartoon character, I screeched into the room. And then I acted nonchalant, as if nothing had happened. The poets welcomed me, handed me a joint, and I sat down splat, already composing a poem entitled "I Stuck My Finger up the Fat Girl's Ass."

I wanted to be the Dorothy Parker of the nineties. I wanted to be the witty, foul-mouthed poetess, with a cigarette in one hand and a martini in the other, soaked in single malt, stirred. But my face was beginning to run like a sad clown's.

In 1997, after a reading in Seattle, I met F. He was interested in poetry and in visiting Canada from the United States of America, so we kept in touch for six months, and then he decided he'd come up for a visit. I made it clear that he could stay for five days tops, so when he arrived and announced that he'd booked his airplane ticket for a twelve-day stay, I felt more than slight aggravation. I had made it equally clear that I was not interested in any intimate interaction, so when he crept into my bedroom in his unwashed boxer shorts the second night of his stay, I was the antithesis of impressed. After three days I was irritated with F.'s whining, bloodsucking and neediness to the marrow of my organism, even imagining ways I might waste the fucker in his sleep.

One of my oldest friends called and invited me to a party. When I told him about my irritating houseguest he laughed and said, "Bring him along." F. was certain he wouldn't like any of my friends, so I dropped him off at a local pub where he could play darts instead. He'd meet me at the party later.

Surprise! It was an engagement party, my worst nightmare. The host, who had made a "never marry" pact with me twenty years previously, was suddenly tying the knot with a bleached-blonde trophy twenty years his junior. The party was jam-packed with dull-brained gold-digging blondettes and beer-bellied divorcés uptight about their steep alimony payments. And with bottles of expensive single-malt Scotch. "Sure. I'll try the rarest first." "Sure, pour me another." My friend announced his engagement with a toast. "Sure, I'll have another." "Sure." How could he break the blood-oath we had made all those years before? We were going to live differently from the rest of the world, he and I, but here he was joining the legions of mediocrity without even forewarning me of his twisted proposal. "Yeah, I'll have another. Make it a triple." My mood was definitely on the rocks.

On my way to the bathroom, I overheard one of the bimbettes telling a prospective husband that she would never have sex before she was married. Bat, bat, bat. Before I had time to think, I turned on my heel and blurted out, "You were a teenaged slut, for Christ's sake, it's written all over you. And now you'd fuck anything that moved for the promise of a ring and a bank account with unlimited credit." The party stopped. I smiled smugly, then retired to the can. As I sat down I noted that (1) I was the only brunette at this saturated soirée, and (2) Maybe I'd gone too far. I giggled to myself. Oh, what the fuck. Flush.

Turns out that little Miss "I'd Never Have Sex Before I Was Married" was the bride-to-be's best friend. Oops. But her prospective husband, enchanted by my swish frankness, invited me to join their group conversation. The blonde gaggle cut an enormously wide berth to accommodate my atrocious mouth. The Scotch had taken hold and I was on a rampage. I held court, telling live sex stories until my friend asked me to leave the party.

Just then F. appeared at the door. On our way outside he grabbed my car keys from my hand. I was incensed, and my late-night visions of murder rose to the surface, but I let him drive. As we passed a corner store, I suggested we stop for cigarettes. "Why don't you come in, and we'll buy some munchies?" I said to F. sweetly.

Once inside, I took the opportunity to punch F. in the head, right beside the potato chips. As he was falling, I grabbed my car keys and cut out of the place. Taking back roads to avoid interference, I drove straight to a friend's place. There was a small group gathered there, and I had them in stitches within seconds.

When I got home the next morning, there was a message from F. He had called the police, who had given him a ride to the airport, and he was thinking of charging me with assault. I phoned him back with a reply threat. My F.U. finger had been broken by the punch, his clothes were already in the dumpster, and I was not in the mood to negotiate.

Three rings in the circus of self-hate, and the circus was getting wilder. I felt beat-up half the time. It was as if I was running behind myself, trying to catch up, calling my own name. "Sheri-D! Wait up!" I was out of breath. Tired. The circus was a nightmare. A blur. Ta-dah! The Sheri-D Show had won, and the real Sheri-D was dead. The blackouts were now so close together there seemed to be no space between them. I had become a sideshow act pierced and branded from head to toe.

I knew by now that my drinking was out of my air-traffic control, but I didn't know how to put myself out of my misery. I knew I wanted the noise to stop, but I couldn't locate the stereo. There had been a time when I had control over the alcohol, and then there was a turning point when alcohol took control over me, completely. Initially the blackouts had happened only when I was drinking. But I had started having gaps in consciousness even when I was sober. Everything had become muted and distorted, as if I were living underwater.

One of my last full-on drinkathons occurred in Montreal. All I remember of that trip is arriving with several thousand dollars and leaving with none. After I quit drinking I ran into several people who saw me at that time, but I have no recollection of them or of the events. One of those people, a poet friend, was still horrified when I bumped into him a year later. He said he'd had to leave the party during my binge-fest in Montreal because he couldn't watch me any more. He told me he'd actually wept. He couldn't bring himself to tell me what he'd witnessed and, to tell the truth, I didn't want to know. When you're playing blackout roulette, it's difficult to remember how many clicks there've been. How many blanks does the gun hold?

I'll never forget that Father's Day morning in 1999 when

I woke up with the taste of poisonous disgust in my mouth. I don't know why it happened that way, on that particular morning, but it wasn't the hangover I felt sick from that day, it was myself. That morning I felt shame for who I had become. I knew I was in big trouble, and I felt ugly to the core. My life no longer seemed humorous or intriguing. I was utterly sick of being sick: sick of puking my guts out into a pail beside my bed every second night; sick of crawling up the front stairs of my building and sleeping on the landing 'cause I couldn't make it to my door; sick of apologizing for things I couldn't remember I'd said and done; sick of the massive phone bills for late-night drunk-o-logues; sick of the excuses and the accidents and the ambulances. But most of all, I felt sick of being someone I wasn't. I was sick of the Sheri-D Show. I wanted to go back to being that crazy eccentric kid from Crocus Road who imagined she was Emma Peel as she played kick the can. That morning I made the commitment to myself that I would stop drinking and start down the slippery path of recovery.

I kicked the physical addiction first, which felt like giving birth to myself. Literally, out of my own asshole. I spent a lot of time walking to release the pain. Now I'm working on the psychological recovery. At times I feel lost, as if I don't know how to do things any more, as if I don't know who I am. At those times, I slow down and remind myself to listen. When I stopped drinking I started to live again, and when I started to live again I started to remember some of what I had forgotten.

Vulnerability is difficult for me after playing the been-there-done-that tough girl for so long. I was worried I'd become soft when I quit and have diddlysquat to write about. As it turns out, the incidents in my life are even more out of the ordinary, with deeper resonance, and now I always have the energy to write.

Finally, I have goosebumps again. For a long time they atrophied, along with the rushes, the surges, the peaks and the valleys. But now they've resurfaced, and the curve of a burnt tree against the sky on a walk along the river, the sound of an undiscovered word, the pause of a deep song all move through me as pure sensation. Sometimes it feels as if my head will blow off. As if I'm being hit by lightning bolt after lightning bolt. Currents rush through me, and I am struck with ekstasis. Without knowing it, that is what I had been looking for all along.

In 2000, the Vancouver writers' festival had a special tribute to the honourable poet P. K. Page. The afternoon was filled with writers telling stories about their associations with Page, most of which involved drinking antics. It wasn't until the poet herself took the stage that the magic was triggered. Standing there in all her elegance and grace, the emerald ring on her walking-stick hand glittering, she read her poetry with the command of a lioness, never raising her voice. A certain alchemy saturated the space, and her words and sounds entered every molecule of my body and soul and mind and heart and I felt as if the top of my head was peeling off my skull. I was worried I might lose my hair with that much energy surging through! I thought I was going to explode on the spot, and I started to shake. As tears rained down, I felt like I needed a drink. There was too much intensity for my body to house. But why bring myself down with booze, I thought, why not experience the fullness of this? That's when I got it—the connection between poetry and love. The circus mask dropped to the ground, and the Sheri-D Show was pronounced dead. I didn't need the image any more. I really was a poet.

Not swimming, but drowning

John Newlove

1.

It was a soft summer night and I was trying to walk the two blocks home from a wedding dance in the community hall. Men with large trays had been going back and forth, offering glasses of the best local home-brew to all takers.

My particular dance was called one step forward, two steps back, fall into the caragana hedge, puke, rest, and try again. At one point as I was lying in the hedge I heard someone walking. The steps stopped and the corner light shone on a pair of black oxfords. A voice said, "Are you all right?"

I puked on the shoes and they went away.

I got home. Details are vague.

In the morning I woke up lying across my bed, partially undressed, stained with and smelling of vomit. I didn't know if I had been caught or not. My mouth was arid and I had a huge, pulsing, soprano headache.

I loved it. I had found what I wanted. I wasn't John the unlikable, unlovable one. I was that other guy, the tough guy with the same name, but drunk. It was freedom.

That's only the booze talking, people used to say.

Funny stuff; but I don't know any other way to tell you what I am.

I knew this was for me, especially the part about not being able to remember anything.

If you can't remember anything then you can do anything, I thought, and it isn't your fault.

I had been caught, of course. I listened meekly to my mother's reproof—God knows that poor dear woman had enough knowledge of drunks to last an eternity—and agreed with her and said I was sorry and it would definitely never happen again, but absent-mindedly, because I was trying to figure out how to get some more booze.

I was a reasonably bright kid, fourteen, too lazy to do homework but bright enough to read the book the day before the provincial exam and get a decent mark, and I was cursed with an argumentative mind that loved what it thought, in its superior teenage way, was logic.

But it was intuition, not logic, told me that so-and-so (the names have been disguised, as they say, to protect the guilty) was weak. Intuition, not logic, told me that if I kept yapping at him he'd buy me a mickey of rye.

It didn't take much intelligence, logic or intuition to realize that in a town of about two thousand people a fourteen-year-old walking around with a case of beer would be noticed. I didn't consider wine; that was for drinking with fancy meals or on fancy occasions, the novels told me, and in the novels no one ever seemed to get drunk.

I wanted to get drunk. I wanted to get pissed out of my head.

I was right about so-and-so. Evil little bastard that I was, I knew once he'd bought me the first bottle he was hooked. What if I told someone? He got me a mickey of rye on a Friday. Because my parents were going to Yorkton Saturday I saved the whisky till then.

Saturday morning I got up, had my breakfast, and wished and wished and wished that they'd hurry up and go to Yorkton.

After they left I had a big slug of the rye and nearly puked again. Puking was looking like something I could get good at. I couldn't skate worth a damn, to this day I don't know the difference between an in-turn and an out-turn; I couldn't dance, or wouldn't; I still have three small spots of lead in my right hand where Karen stabbed me with a pencil after I tried to grab her largely theoretical tits in Grade 9; and I had a bad mouth and flew into screaming, sobbing rages I could never see coming on and if I got clocked in a fight it didn't matter, because nothing could hurt me.

I would have been one hell of a small-town Saskatchewan-style defenceman if my skating had been a better.

(Oh Karen, lost, never realized darling I was so afraid of, I asked about you in 1980 and they told me you were fat, and this isn't even your real name.)

Once I mastered my gorge I drank the rest of the rye as quickly as I could—it wasn't anything like as good as the local home-brew—and puked on the nasturtiums. I hid the empty mickey in a culvert and walked down to Peter's Pool Palace and breathed on people.

"Jesus, have you got a skinful," one kid said. "Where'd you get it?" "Ask me no questions, I'll tell you no lies," I said. We never actually talked—at least I didn't—but it didn't matter much because none of us trusted closeness and we had an encyclopedia of pat phrases designed to push people away.

When my parents came home in the early evening it was obvious I'd been drinking. My mother gave me The Look and went into the front room to confront my father.

"Harold," she said, "you've got to talk to that boy."

"What can I say," he said.

He was a drunk too. He was a man I remember seeing only on odd occasions, briefly, before I was ten, in three of the small Saskatchewan towns where my mother taught. My guess is that my mother loved him dearly but wouldn't put up with his drunkenness; attempts at living together must have failed many times.

In Veregin, when I was in Grade 4, my mother was the principal of the local two-building, three-room public and high school. My father had set up a new law practice in Kamsack, nine or ten miles away. He lived there weekdays. On weekends he came to stay in Veregin and whipped the shit out of me.

I knew, or I thought I knew, that I had been an unwanted baby, an accident. I made up stories. I convinced myself that my mother and father had had an earlier child, about the same age as my much older brother and sister, with exactly my name, and that I was just a replacement for him. Because, unlike most of the people I saw, my father seemed to think that Indians were human beings, I convinced myself that I was a Saulteaux orphan they had adopted.

And so on and so on. I couldn't be real. It was clear to me that though I was capable of loving desperately, I myself was unlovable.

There you are. I stood in the high-school gym during sock dances feeling sorry for myself.

At least self-pity is never a false emotion.

One weekend my father came home sober and he never drank again. He'd been to AA and it worked. He was a stubborn bastard. I admired him. I still do. He wouldn't take Communion because he was afraid that even that small taste of wine would set him off.

Much later my mother told me that when she came to my little room in Veregin to kiss me good-night on my father's first sober Saturday I asked her who that man was.

2.

I was registered at the University of Saskatchewan for a year but I had to pass pubs on the way to classes. I had my first draft beer at the Senator. We go grey early in my family and I'd had some grey in my hair since I was sixteen or seventeen: not tragedies, not heartbreak, just genetics. I thought it might get me by.

The Senator had two levels. I went to the top one because there was no one else there, sat down and put a five-dollar bill on the table. My intuitive, intelligent, logical mind had never gotten around to asking anybody what draft beer cost, but I knew five bucks would cover it easily; then I could count the change and figure it out. A bored waiter came over and put two draft on the table. I eased the five-dollar bill toward him. He made change (he'd given me two big glasses, twenty cents each) and I dropped a dime into his hand.

I had a mouthful of beer. I thought, Okay, I can do this any time. I looked around. The waiter was leaning against the wrought-iron railing that divided the lower and upper floors. He was watching me. When he saw that I was watching him too he came over and put my draft back on his tray. I thought, Oh shit. He said, "Follow me," and I did. He went to a two-man (no women allowed) table behind a big pillar, put my draft on it and said, "Sit here, sonny. Nobody can see you here."

3.

Then I had various jobs, for most of which I was not qualified; but one thing you learn early as a drunk is that you've got to be able to talk your way out of any of the shit you've landed in, and that doesn't demand anything but charm. I found out that I could put it on, so I added charm as one more thing on my list of stuff not to trust. In the meantime, I was a high-school teacher, a social worker (public assistance, not a baby snatcher), a continuity writer and announcer for three small Saskatchewan radio stations and, when I couldn't avoid it, a ditchdigger, warehouseman, swamper and general asshole.

I made my voice deep.

4.

My life consisted of one desire only. Get pissed. Get out of it.

"She's a pig, man, and she's stupid, too. How can you do it with her? You got no self-respect, man," a friend said in a beer parlour somewhere.

He was right, but I won. "She buys me booze, man," I said. "You're drinking her money right now."

"Point," he said. "But I'm just glad I don't have to fuck her."

"I'm no prize either," I said. "One of these days I'm going to tell her who I'm pretending it is if she'll tell me who she's pretending it is. In the meantime let's get the hell out of it."

5.

No problem. I could stop right now if I wanted to. No problem. But I don't want to.

6.

Years later in Nelson, B.C., when my wife was away—I think she was away—I did stop.

Before you can go into the addicts' floor in the hospital you have to have been dry for seven days. After the bars had closed I went home and knocked myself out with a forty-ouncer of Ballantine's and whatever beer was around. I collapsed on the chesterfield. When I woke up I drifted off and woke up and drifted off and started to shake and I thought, This is bullshit, I can do this any time. I just don't want to do it now. But it was the middle of the night, as my logical mind had thought it might be, and I didn't know any bootleggers.

When I woke up fully it was because the phone was ringing. I fell off the chesterfield and crawled over to the phone and picked it up. It was my doctor, Liz, and she was worried about me because I'd told her what I was going to try. She'd phoned to tell me that she'd tried to get me a hospital bed so she could sedate me, but no beds were available. One of the loony premiers of British Columbia was busily saving the taxpayers of the province, who at the time included me at a fairly high level, money by shutting down hospital beds.

Liz once said she could not understand how someone as intelligent as I was could do this to myself.

Intelligence has nothing to do with it.

Okay. I was very thirsty and I was starting to have convulsions. I wanted to crawl to the bathroom. I figured I'd be able to turn on the cold-water tap in the bath and slurp up some water like a dog.

Dogs. I couldn't go that way because in the corner blocking me off was a big white St. Bernard with its chest a sheet of fresh wet blood and it was smiling at me. I got to the kitchen instead and managed to spill a package of sugar on the floor and licking it up got my saliva running.

Let me tell you about the medical profession. Never go to a male doctor. The guy who admitted me to the addicts' floor in Nelson gave me a full-blown God-to-a-little-black-beetle moral lecture and then a very rough physical exam, including an anal examination that amounted to a rape.

Rape must be fun if you don't like love, or even sex.

An emergency-room doctor who stitched up my mouth one time told me, when I said to him afterwards, "That wasn't much of a painkiller you gave me," "I never give painkillers to drunks."

Male nurses are more forgiving than females nurses are, though. Female nurses, like male GPS, know that you are doing this to harass them when they've got people who are really sick to look after and you can stop any time you want to stop: it's a moral problem.

Specialists don't matter much because you're just a thing to them.

7.

Clinically, pancreatitis is one result of alcoholism. The pancreas gives up in despair and refuses to process your food. My doctor in Ottawa was English and she weighed me on an old imperial scale. When I got to 134 pounds from 195 she said, "You have a very strong constitution, Mr. Newlove. Why don't you give it a chance?"

I discovered that if you have water handy and some sour-lemon candies to keep your mouth wet, starving to death is a good way to die. You lose interest. You sleep a lot.

A specialist later told me that pancreatitis is very difficult to diagnose, and that what seems like back pain is caused by this little bit of specialized meat spewing out angry juices into the surrounding organs.

Of course, I have back pain on its own.

My English doctor had a total body bone scan done on me— why don't they put television on the ceilings of those cold white rooms for the occasions when you have to lie still for forty minutes?—and she told me I had cracked or broken at least one representative bone in every part of my body, from the right collarbone down.

I said, "I've never broken my collarbone."

"Yes, you have," she said. "See. In two places."

8.

I have seen W sober, but not often. The last time I saw him it was wintertime in Saskatoon and he didn't know what city he was in.

I have never seen X, Y or Z sober.

The last time I saw X we had bailed him out of the drunk tank in the Vancouver Public Safety Building. It had been a close thing but even in the cells he had managed somehow to stay drunk, and now that he was out he was putting a high polish on it.

The last time I saw Y he was being squeezed out a barely open fire door in an Edmonton beer parlour by a very large Cree woman he'd been mouthy to.

The last time I saw Z a friend and I were beating him up at a party. The woman I was with went into the kitchen and told my friend's wife, "John and Mike are beating up Z." Mike's wife said, "Oh, everybody does that."

I have to assume that all four are dead, long dead.

Strange shapes that piss in the night . . .

9.

I'm a drunk and here's one of those not-so-funny riddles about me.

It asks, How can you tell when a drunk's lying?

Answer: His lips move; or his fingers move shakily over the keyboard.

God, I love it.

10.

I think it begins at about age fourteen, give or take a year. I think the child is desperate to be loved, or at least to be noticed. I think the child loves deeply but thinks it is not loveable. I think the child feels it is an afterthought, a mistake.

This child is an only one or is in the situation of an only one. Unique.

Not like the others. Therefore, wrong, hardly human, a performer with no audience, a fake.

It loves its mother and father desperately but nothing they can ever do will convince it that the love is returned.

(Like many young men for a long time I thought I was tougher than I really was, and like many men for a long time I thought I was younger than I really was. I hurt a lot of people I didn't want to hurt, including myself.)

Nothing anyone can do will convince it. It is determined to be a victim.

It doesn't want to be here, to be in this life of pain and shame.

Now I understand who I have been trying to punish all my life, but that is no excuse.

I still don't like to be touched.

11.

When I came downstairs my mother said, "You've been drinking, John."

I said, "They made me do it."

She said, "Nobody makes you drink, John. You do."

My thanks to Lorna Crozier for confirming that the title I have used here was stolen from Stevie Smith. I misremembered the original, which is "Not waving, but drowning."

Junkie

Stephen Reid

The blood broke into two rivulets along the smooth skin of my inner forearm. My head sank back into the new leather of the bucket seat and my body went limp. Paul returned the glass syringe to its coffinlike case and dabbed at my arm with a soft white cotton ball. His face swam up to mine, as if to steal a kiss. I felt such a helpless peace I would have kissed him back, had I known how. On that warm Indian-summer day in northern Ontario, I had just been given my first taste of morphine. I wouldn't turn twelve until the snow fell and melted again the following spring; by then I would have had a lot more of Paul and a lot more of his morphine. By then, I'd have learned to fix myself.

Paul was everything I was not. He was rich, had elegant features and graceful hands. He owned a new white Thunderbird convertible. Paul was also a grown man, a doctor and a pedophile. The morphine, of course, was a prelude.

Something was loosed in me that October day, something beyond blood, beyond my bantam genitals from my jeans. There is a memory so fixed and so perfect that on certain days a part of my brain listens to no other. *The top is down on his Thunderbird, the pale autumn sun warm on my skin. The blood running down my arm is like spilled roses. We are hidden from the road, partway down an old tractor trail in the grass. I am pressed against the rich red leather. Not ten feet away, yellow waxy leaves make their death rattle in the late-afternoon breeze. I am in profound awe of the ordinary—the pale sky, the blue spruce tree, the rusty barbed-wire fence, those dying yellow leaves. I am high. I am eleven years old and in communion with this world. Wholly innocent, I enter the heart of unknowing.*

For much of the winter that followed I lay face down on the couch in Paul's rec room, with my skinny white arm sticking out from under him, waiting for the next jab. I still lived at home, shared a bed with my brother, and ate my porridge with brown sugar every morning at the crowded kitchen table. I carried myself to school. After dinner, I slung my hockey bag over my shoulder and left the house waving to my mother, who thought I was spending my evenings at the rink. I can still see Paul's car, idling, with the lights out, waiting for me on the snow-packed road, the plume of the car's exhaust rising in the cold air, a curtain of white vapour I crossed through each time I went to him. That was the winter I began to disappear from my life.

Day-to-day existence became like an old photograph, faded and curling in at the edges. My body, once eager to explore every nook and cranny of the world around me, seemed now to resist the smallest of efforts. I went to Paul again and again, trying to get *me* back, trying to jam *me* back up my veins. But the more I tried, the more gaping the hole became, until so much had been spilled from me only the morphine seemed to matter. The struggle to stop my boyhood from flowing out changed to a struggle to stem the darkness flooding in—the secret self-loathing that pools in the heart of every junkie.

Paul unzipped my childhood, but it's never been as singular or as uncomplicated as blame. Mine is more than the story of a boy interrupted. It is not what Paul took from me, it is what I kept: the lie that the key to the gates of paradise was a filled syringe. In all the thousands of syringes I've emptied into my arm since then, the only gates that ever opened led to the penitentiary. Yet for most of my adult years I have clung to a deep sense of longing, a desire to return to that moment when the plunger hit bottom and the morphine arrived home for the very first time. I have staggered through a turbulent life, but I've lived that life in the arena of possibilities like everyone else. I have made countless choices along the way, broken my bones on good fortune, vandalized the best of my intentions. I have misappropriated trust, defrauded love, and found—then lost—redemption so many times you'd think I had holes in my pockets, all the while trying desperately to transport myself back to that first taste of radiance, to obliterate the dark winter that followed.

I have quit heroin to become a better thief. I have quit

heroin to become a better father, a better husband, a better friend, a better citizen. I have maintained these clean and good intentions for years at a stretch, but I have never stayed quit. It's true of men: we keep our dark secrets, hold to an unflagging belief in our manly self-will. We don't ask for directions to the corner store, and we don't ask for help in our lives. I have always returned to the needle and the spoon with a childish thirst, a self-centred insistence that I can attain utopia. The voice of the addict whispers, "Come this way, it will be different this time. Just this once, what you seek will be here." *Ad*, from the Latin "toward" or "yes," and *dict*, from the Latin "say." Addicts just say yes.

There is a Zen-like irony in the junkie slang "to fix." A shot of heroin doesn't fix anything: heroin only gives shelter to that which is broken. Blaise Pascal, the French philosopher, wrote, "Every action involves risk, possibly loss, all action leads to pain." In plainer terms: Nobody moves, and nobody gets hurt. Heroin addicts want to stop the world from spinning, to fix a point in time where it is safe—an embryonic state, the place before loss.

There were nine children in our family. One died young. We moved a lot when I was growing up. The houses we rented, like the town, seemed always too small; my mother had too little money to raise too many kids. My father was away much of the time: first the Army, then the northern lumber camps, then the mines. When he came home he drank hard with his "chums," and they made the kitchen seem even smaller. I loved my dad fiercely, from the misspelled name he had tattooed on his arm the day I was born to the callouses on his hands. And I believe he loved me back in the only way he knew how. My dad would have killed Paul, but the fury he would have saved for me is what kept me silent.

At thirteen I began riding a yellow bus to the regional high school nineteen miles down Highway 17. At first the school, my circle of friends, had the gloss and mystery of newness. I attached myself to this fresh town with zeal, spending as little time as possible at home.

My secret life with Paul got easier. His house—with its plush carpets, art on the walls, a refrigerator rich with food and not one but two big, shiny bathrooms—was mere blocks from my new school. I hitchhiked home only to sleep. My dad remained absent, in one way or another, and my mom was buried under piles of laundry. I slipped away to become the ghost of my own boyhood.

Being from my hometown was like being from a bad neighbourhood. I parlayed that image into as much leather-jacket mystique as I could among the sons and daughters of merchants and mill managers. These were boys who worried about their golf scores and wore machine-knitted sweaters over houndstooth slacks. The girls had ponytails and wore Ban-Lon sweaters tucked into plaid skirts. They put pennies in their loafers and Kleenex in their brassieres.

We guzzled mickeys of lemon gin, those boys and me, in the washroom at school dances. I drank to wash down the black beauties and christmas trees I stole from Paul's bag of tricks. The gin helped kill the taste of him; the uppers quelled the nausea. When the dances ended, I would be fighting outside the New Moon Restaurant or walking one of those plaid-skirted girls home. On the sofas in their parents' living rooms, I kissed those girls too hard, then stole their mothers' tranquilizers from the medicine cabinet on my way out the door.

Paul took a vacation to Mexico and returned with poolside pictures and a bag of marijuana. He was growing leery of giving me more morphine and, I think, tiring of me. But nothing could shake my determination to extract more from him. An unspoken blackmail hung in the air between us.

Each time Paul gave me the hard stuff he'd write something in a ledger that he left on the bar. One night, high and curious, I peeked. The ledger turned out to be a mandatory account of narcotic dispensations he was obliged to keep for the RCMP. Paul had been falsely recording every cc of morphine he'd shot into me as injections to his patients.

The next day in class I kept staring at my friend Bobby M., wondering if he knew his mother was dying, afraid he'd find out I'd taken the medicine meant for her. I began to fear that everyone would learn about me and Paul. It was like living with an execution date. I started to fragment. One spring morning I missed the yellow bus. I crossed the asphalt highway and stuck out my thumb to cars heading west.

I landed on the West Coast three years too early for the Summer of Love. In the dark heart of downtown Vancouver I had instead my first summer of heroin. In those few short months I would learn ninety-nine names for junk and lose the one for love.

Main and Hastings, the Corner: I wasn't there a hot five minutes before a young native guy turned me around so his pal could steal my gym bag. The slim contents must have evoked some feeling of kinship, because I hardly had time to notice the bag missing before they were handing it back. The first guy put his fist under my nose and told me they called him "Box," because that's what he liked to do.

Box took me for coffee at the Plaza Cafe, where there were tiny holes in the bottom of all the spoons. Box filled me in: the Chinese proprietor drilled his spoons to discourage the dope-fiend clientele from stealing them or using them to cook up in his washroom. The cops kicked the toilet doors off their hinges on a regular basis.

I'd barely had time to stir my coffee when a character everyone seemed to be waiting for strolled in the door. He wore a green suit, and his hair looked like it had been licked by a cat. Teddy Beaver was a bundle player who oversaw a small network of singles dealers. A bundle, I would learn in the weeks to come, was a package of twenty-five #5 capsules of heroin, triple-tied in a prophylactic, called a stall. I also would learn to carry the stall in my mouth, ready to swallow it at the first sign of a roust. In those days, simple possession meant a certain trip to the penitentiary.

There was a code on the Corner back then: strangers and children couldn't buy heroin. Ray Charles could see I was no cop, but Teddy wasn't going to be responsible for me being "turned out." Even after I had rolled up my sleeve and showed how Paul had already taken care of that, Teddy said he didn't want me catching a habit on his dope. It didn't matter. Box scored off Teddy, and I was "in the car."

Box scurried back to his flop with me so tight on his tail we made one shadow on the scarred red bricks along the alley. We took the back stairs of the Balmoral Hotel two at a time and hit the one john shared by all the tenants of the second floor. There was a round hole where the lock should have been; I braced my foot against the bottom of the door the way Box showed me to and kneeled to keep six out the peephole.

Box worked quickly, removing a bent spoon, an eye-dropper and the steel point of a needle he had hidden in the toilet-paper tube. He cooked the dope until the water fried at the edges of the spoon, then sat on the toilet and twisted his shirtsleeve into a knot over his bicep. When the veins jumped up, he held the dropper like a dart and sunk the needle into his arm.

Blood flagged into the dropper, and Box squeezed the bulb. His eyes closed and his body slumped against the toilet tank, the needle still hanging from his arm. I shouted his name. When he wouldn't respond, I started to shake him. Box gradually came around enough to repeat the whole cooking ritual, and this time he sunk the needle into my wing.

We spent the remains of the day in his room, sprawled across the sagging bed listening to a scratchy Chet Baker record. My tolerance was low, and I about went to heaven on less than a quarter cap. Box didn't get seasick, but me, I ran to the bathroom and spewed my junkie bile every half-hour or so.

I entered the world of Hastings Street with all the zest of a kid joining the carny. Box and I shoplifted meat and sold it to the five o'clock crowd at the Blackstone. We dry-tricked the fags over on Seymour, hustling them for ten bucks with a promise to appear. A ten-dollar bill was known as a sawbuck, the currency of the Corner. It was what the hookers charged; the price of a blow job was tied to the cost of a single cap of heroin. Box and I did whatever it took to go back to the Balmoral and get high.

Teddy Beaver appeared on the Corner every afternoon about three and stood there surveying his kingdom. One day he overheard Box ragging on me about rent. He led me by the elbow to a back booth at the Plaza for a mano a mano. I went to work for Teddy. Whenever one of his singles dealers needed to be re-upped, I would make the pickup, then the delivery. I was handling twelve to sixteen bundles a day, three hundred to four hundred caps, and yet I still couldn't score on my own.

Teddy put me away with a hooker called Kitty, whose old

man had, until his court appearance that morning, worked for him. He was now sitting out a deuce-less in Oakalla. I retrieved my gym bag from Box's room and waited at the Plaza for Kitty-Cat to finish her shift. She scored two caps and we hailed a cab, stopping on Davie Street at the all-night pharmacy. KC kissed me to pass me the stall, then clip-clopped inside to grab a new kit—one eyedropper and a #26 point.

Kitty had a one-bedroom in a six-storey building on Bute. She started apologizing for the place while we were still in the elevator. Kitty was a serial apologist; she was still saying her sorrys through the bedroom door while I rummaged in her kitchen drawers for a spoon. I had cooked up and fixed half a cap before she came out in a housecoat. Kitty stood short in flat-bottomed slippers and was every inch a tender mess. I hesitated when she asked me to cook her up one cap—a cap fix was a major habit, one that would kill most users—but then I threw it in the spoon.

Before I got even half the whack into her, Kitty was into an overdose. She turned blue. I wrestled her limp body into a cold shower, where she came around slowly. It turned out Kitty's ex had been "giving her the Fraser River." It was an old junkie double-cross, which in New York would be called giving somebody the Hudson; in Toronto, Lake Erie. Kitty thought she had a major habit, but she had been shooting mostly water while her boyfriend "h.o.'d" the dope for himself.

Kitty and I fell into a routine. We kept vampire hours.

Every day we woke to the setting sun, did a jimmy-hix; then she put on her high heels and painted her mouth target-red. I put on my sneakers and we caught a cab to the Corner. She went to work at the Blackstone, me to the Plaza Cafe.

Kitty became the mirror I was afraid to look into. The heroin had us both by the throat, and I watched her skin turn grey, her bones start to jut, and sores develop at the corner of her mouth. We began to resemble the other zombie dope fiends, spiritless, single-minded in our obsession. The search for pleasure devolved into the avoidance of withdrawal. If I went without heroin for more than a few hours my nose would drip and my legs begin to ache. My quest for utopia had become a ritual of drudgery, the daily grind to maintain a habit.

One night on our way home, after she had scored our dope, Kitty announced she was pregnant. I didn't know how. She turned French tricks exclusively, and I was using four caps a day; for all the erections I ever got, she could have had swallows nesting in her vagina and I wouldn't have known. In the elevator my legs wobbled and I got a bitter taste in my mouth. The alarm bells went off, and I spit out an eight-cap stall as I slid to the floor. True to junkie form, Kitty went for the stall before she tried to help me to my feet. The stall she had forgotten to triple-tie.

I woke in St. Paul's Hospital looking up at the gentle face of a nurse. She was touching the tracks on my arms and crying. I closed my eyes, then snuck out as soon as she left the

room. I waited in a blue gown at a bus stop across the street
for Kitty to come pick me up in a cab. I sat on that bench,
fourteen years old and so hollowed out I didn't even understand why that nurse had been so sad.

Teddy was a no-show one night, and a minor panic set in
until Jerry the German went out to Chilliwack and came back
with an o-zee already capped up. The word on the street next
day was Teddy had been shot eight times and stuffed down a
sewer grate. Rumours flew. Some said it was the Roadrunner,
a notoriously vicious cop; others said Teddy had double-
doored the Chinese Triads. Whatever the truth, his mother,
an old east-end matriarch, spent two days and two nights out
in the pouring rain, searching, until she came to the one
manhole cover she hadn't wanted to find. They say the old
lady lifted Teddy's body out by herself.

Kitty scored me the first bundle I could call my own. I began
putting out singles from a booth in the White Lunch. One
night I was tucking a twenty in my sock, having just sold two
caps to Donny-the-Poet, when two harness bulls walked in
and pinned him to the floor. Behind them came the Roadrunner. He usually carried a wedge-handled flashlight to pry
open the mouth of a reluctant hype, but this time he wasn't in
the mood for formalities. When Donny wouldn't spit out the
stall, the other two cops held him down while the Roadrunner coolly bent a fork around his own hand and began to

dig his way into the Poet's mouth. Before Donny could surrender, his lips were hanging in so many shreds his mouth
looked like the entrance to a car wash. On his way out, the
Roadrunner warned me to sit tight, he'd be back.

I phoned Kitty from San Francisco a few weeks later.
She'd had a miscarriage and was home from the hospital. The
Roadrunner had come looking for me and had hung her by
the ankles from the balcony. She said when he let go of her all
she could think of was how glad she was she hadn't gotten the
fifth-floor apartment she'd always wanted. The next time I
called, her number was out of service.

I was arrested that fall outside Berkeley with a tobacco
pouch full of third-grade marijuana. A judge declared me a
juvenile non grata; I was flown to Seattle to await expulsion
from the country. On the trip from the airport to King
County Jail, in the back of the prison van, a black man tried
to force me to masturbate him. We were both cuffed, and my
struggles to keep him at bay amused the sheriffs no end.

The next morning an FBI agent drove me to the border
crossing and turned me over to Canada Customs and Immi-
gration. They left me unattended in a waiting room, and I
bolted. I caught a ride to Vancouver and phoned my Uncle
Victor, who wired me enough money to buy a ticket on the
first Greyhound bus back to northern Ontario.

My mother hugged me for ten minutes straight, but it
was a week before my dad acknowledged my presence in the
house. I returned to school, ready to repeat the year I had

missed, but my determination began to dissolve in the sea of faces in that Grade 9 classroom. My small-town values, my human values, had been forever altered. I knew things no fourteen-year-old should have to know. The days of catching snowflakes on my tongue were over.

Within months I was gone again. I got as far as Winnipeg, where I was arrested for shoplifting a leather jacket from the Bay and put in the Public Safety Building. I had a cellblock to myself. For a week I saw only a hand that set a cup of coffee and a muffin on my bars in the morning and coffee and a sandwich at lunch and dinner. Then I was sent home. My mother hugged me, my father ignored me. The ink hadn't dried on my probation papers before I was back out on the highway, my thumb hooked in the general direction of Toronto. Over the next few years, I returned to live with my parents for shorter and shorter periods. Sometimes I was brought home in the back of an OPP cruiser, sometimes I came on my own because I felt too beat-up out there.

On one trip home I learned Paul had been caught with his hands down a pair of houndstooth pants. Paul had made a mistake messing with one of their own, and the town fathers had sent him packing. During another short stay I went back to the place where Paul had parked his Thunderbird and given me my first taste, near the old Woolgemuth farm. I even fixed heroin there, in the futile hope that whatever portal had been opened on that long-ago afternoon would be opened for me again.

At sixteen I found myself back in Vancouver, back on the Corner. Two years had gone by, but I entered into the rhythm of the street so quickly you'd think I'd only been to the bathroom. I heard that Kitty had dropped some Purple Rain and gone to Haight-Ashbury to find herself. I spent Christmas that year in the solitary cells under the old cow barns in Oakalla prison for selling some bunk pot to an undercover agent.

Once I got out I went back east again, to London, where I took up with a hooker named Big Julie and acquired a methamphetamine habit. When shooting crystal got too weird, I found myself another nurse who cried over the tracks on my arms. When she ran out of tears and went back to her life, I took my madness to Toronto. Wired to the yin-yang on a $500-a-day habit, I picked up a Saturday night special.

Before Christmas of 1970, I was charged with three bank robberies. The holdup squad had beaten me so badly I had to be arraigned in early-morning magistrates' court wearing a garbage bag over my head. Don Jail officials turned me away at the front gate—I was sent to St. Michael's Hospital instead, where my jaw was wired, my broken teeth pulled, my forehead sutured, and my ribs strapped back into place. After two weeks of being handcuffed to a hospital bed, I was returned to the Don and admitted. The doctor waiting to do my intake medical, in a joyless cinderblock room, was Paul. I had heard he'd recently received five years for sexual assault and administering a narcotic to a minor, and I gathered he was being made to serve his sentence as a somewhat glorified orderly. He sat behind a bare table, wearing an ugly white smock, and went down the perfunctory checklist, never raising his eyes from my file photograph, asking questions in a monotone. When we were done he didn't ask me if I was in any pain, and I didn't ask him for any morphine. A month shy of my twenty-first birthday, a judge handed me ten years in Canada's oldest prison, Kingston Penitentiary.

My second night in the pen an old dope fiend named Suitcase Simpson hooked me up with a handful of pills. The head keeper saw me crossing the dome on the wobble and sway and ran me straight to the hole. He charged me for "condition other than normal," or CON for short. It was a charge I would see frequently, and a condition I would aspire to, for the next few years.

Prisons are about addictions. Most prisoners are casualties of their habits. They have all created victims—some in cruel and callous ways—but almost to a man they have first practised that cruelty on themselves. Prison provides the loneliness that fuels addiction. It is the slaughterhouse for addicts, and all are eventually delivered to its gates.

When we were lucky and got a package in, we used homemade rigs—syringes made from ballpoint pens and coat hangers. Other times we cooked down Darvons and cough syrup from the infirmary, or stole yeast and tomato juice from the kitchen to make a brew. We did what we could to get past the four corners of our cells.

Eventually I was transferred to a medium-security facility. I decided to throw the dope to the ground and look for another kind of escape. Within eight months I had a hook 'n' ladder play together and was living the life of a fugitive in Ottawa, where I met Paddy Mitchell and Lionel Wright; the three of us became known as the Stopwatch Gang. For the next dozen or so years, heroin ceased to be at the centre of my universe. I sipped whisky to soothe the beast, but I was too busy to chase a dope habit. We stole millions of dollars, racked up nine escapes among the three of us, and made the most wanted list in two countries. By Hallowe'en of 1980 the FBI had caught up with me in Arizona. They dragged me off to the ultimate penitentiary: Marion, Illinois.

Four years later I was transferred to Canada. I had grown bone-weary of prison culture and my criminal lifestyle. I went to my cell one day, closed my door, and began to write. When my head came up a year later, I had the first draft of a novel. I sent the manuscript to Fred Desroches, a criminologist at the University of Waterloo, who passed it on to their writer-in-residence, Susan Musgrave. Susan became my editor, then my wife, in a maximum-security wedding. I published *Jackrabbit Parole*, and a year later I was released.

We moved to Vancouver Island, to a vine-covered cottage by the sea. I bought a weed eater, and a pink bicycle for my stepdaughter, Charlotte. I planted annuals. I began to engage with a new matrix of friends; I planted perennials. For the first two years I fixed up our home, pounding nails and painting trim. Susan and I had a second daughter, Sophie. I began another novel but found myself staring for hours at a blank page. I had been released from prison, but still I had not escaped. I felt the same profound aloneness in the midst of my warrant-burning party in our garden as I had in my Grade 9 class. Once again I went in search of the only solace I knew.

The only real serenity I have ever experienced, paradoxically and tellingly, has been without the assistance of drugs. It arose from a long period of abstinence, late in life, encouraged by the love of my wife and my daughters, nurtured by my friends, and witnessed by a God of my understanding—in whom, ultimately, I could not extinguish my addiction.

Even after a lifetime, I was not done with my crimes, nor were they done with me. In 1999 I returned to a full-blown heroin and cocaine habit. I had tried to keep a foot in each world, to hold onto the weight of love and family, but I was pulled into the underworld of drugs. I chose to destroy both lives—not in a calculated way, more by default, but a choice nonetheless. I committed the worst bank robbery of my life, an unprofessional, unnecessary act of violence. It cost me an eighteen-year sentence, and nearly cost some people their lives.

Now, at fifty pieces, I find myself stripped bare, beaten back from hope, all out of illusions, in yet another prison cell. Having fallen through the crust of this earth so many times, it seems that only on this small and familiar pad of concrete, where I can make seven steps in one direction, then take seven back, do my feet touch down with any certainty.

A year before my arrest, when Sophie was nine, we went out sliding after a freak snowfall. Hurtling down the hill on a red plastic saucer, we whirled faster and faster until the edge caught and we spilled. We tumbled through the snow, Sophie's pearly whites shining to the heavens, her laughter like small golden bells.

Now Sophie is twelve. When she accompanies her mother on their weekly visits to the prison, I hold her on my lap, and those wide brown eyes fix onto mine. Sophie needs to see me rise up again, return to her life. Though we are connected in unbreakable ways, I worry about her memories of a drug-addicted dad.

So I pace, seven steps one way, seven steps back. And I write. The days pass. I sit on my concrete pad, cross my legs, and begin to breathe. The darkness of my world melts away, and as I move toward the mystery of mysteries, I can almost hear those faint golden bells. Slowly I enter the heart of un-knowing, without expectation, without heroin.

Afterword

⁓

A MONTH AFTER I wrote my essay for this book I lay in my front hall, flopping on the hardwood floor like a salmon on the bottom of a boat. Two days later I went into a residential treatment program. For the next eight weeks, I spent sixteen hours a day stumbling through group therapy, AA meetings, confused sessions with my counsellor, and endless conversations with other drunks and addicts.

Every morning in that place I got up into the last of night so I could drink thin coffee and have a cigarette outside in the smoke pit, alone except for the watchful night staff and a few ghostly inmates who walked the halls mumbling to themselves. One early morning I saw a full moon as I walked the narrow path from my room to the main building to begin another hopeless day. I was detoxed, but I didn't know who I was. I knew I wasn't in prison, yet it felt like it. I knew I could walk away any time I wanted, yet I was afraid, terrified of leaving. I remember stopping in the middle of the path and looking up at that pale fire in the sky. It was just the moon, you understand. Yet I remember standing there, still, and then I lifted my arms and said to the night and the stars and that glistening, distant moon: I give up. I surrender.

And I did.

After almost fifty years of addiction I was finished.

The essays in this collection are not confessions. It would be too easy to call them that. Maybe each is a kind of witnessing to a life lived at both ends of a burning candle. If the words help someone survive, then this book will do what Lorna Crozier and I want it to.

Last December, the first of the millennium, the *Globe and Mail* asked me to write a piece about Christmas. I was barely a week out of treatment and still pretty shaky. I include the piece here to remind myself of who I've been and who I am now. I think of the people I went through treatment with. Today, seven months later, six of them are dead, and the plaque on the wall of the treatment centre reads a little longer.

The world calls us drunks and addicts. The people here call us chemically dependent. What we call ourselves is mostly unprintable. The counsellors tell us we have a disease. The woman next to me, a sweet nineteen-year-old, is an anorexic heroin addict who's been hooking on the street since she was eleven. Beside her is a young man who started dealing crack cocaine in Grade 8 to pay for his habit. He was on the street at fifteen, selling his body every few hours for a hundred or fifty or sometimes twenty quick bucks and beaten a hundred times in rooms and alleys. The drunks are older. It can sometimes take a while to hit bottom from liquor. But most of the drunks are addicted to other things as well: crystal meth, Ecstasy, Tylenol 3, Valium, amphetamines, hash, crack cocaine, heroin.

We're all standing around a forty-foot Christmas tree singing carols, something we didn't do when we were lying in our lonely rooms with a bottle, a pipe or a needle. We're here for seven or eight weeks or longer. Some of us will stay for a year or more. Right now none of us are thinking of the plaque on the wall outside listing the dead addicts and drunks who came through here. We're singing Christmas carols as loud as we can and drinking pop, coffee or tea as we stare at the tree, that old pagan image of the solstice. Some of us will be dead in six weeks or six months and some of us will live a while longer. It's Christmas in treatment and the only family we have is us, our shared disease, this addiction that has driven us past despair to this place of compassion and confrontation.

We sing "Jingle Bells" and follow it with "The First Noël." Most of us are tough people who can laugh or cry at will. Con artists, naive dreamers, romantics and fools, most of us have lived on the street at one time or another, but here, in this season of apprehended joy, there is just a hope there might be something more than what we've got. Around us are the whispers of the past, families and loved ones, some of whom still care and some who can't any more. But the season here isn't sad. We're too frightened to be sad, too frightened to be lonely.

We sing as hard as we can. The tree glistens with lights. There is a strange, surreal happiness in the room. It is a time for song and no one thinks of the night to come, the stunned tears in the dark, the fear that moves hidden among us. A boy-man beside me sings along to "Rudolph, the Red-Nosed Reindeer" and we all join in with laughter at how silly we are. Yesterday was the first time this man wore a short-sleeved shirt. White scars crawl like worms on his arms. He is getting past his shame.

A young woman hiding behind a post sings softly, shyly, with her eyes half closed. She is someone's daughter, someone's lover. I would take her hand if I could. I would tell her everything will be all right. But I can't do that. The odds are things won't be okay ever again. She's only a step away from a room of crack pipes and seizures, a broken bottle in the back seat of a car, a needle hanging from her arm. She's only a step away from being clean, too, but that's a big step, and I don't know if she'll take it.

It's Christmas. There's a tree and many lights and people singing. Some of us will make it, some of us won't, but we sing our hearts out anyway. We sing as hard as we can.

—Patrick Lane

About the Contributors

Books in Canada has called **Lorna Crozier** one of the most original poets writing today. Her books have received every national accolade, including the prestigious Governor General's Award. Born in Saskatchewan, she presently teaches at the University of Victoria. She is the editor of *Desire in Seven Voices* and, with Patrick Lane, of the acclaimed poetry anthology *Breathing Fire*. Her most recent book is *What the Living Won't Let Go*.

Peter Gzowski has been the editor of more magazines than many people have read, the host of more radio and TV programs than many people have listened to or watched, and the embarrassed recipient of more lifetime achievement awards than most people have lifetimes. Father of five, grandfather of two, he was the winner of an East Coast Music Award (mostly for not singing during the breaks) and once came second in one of his own golf tournaments for literacy, which are now held in all ten provinces and all three territories of Canada. He has never been to Zagreb but has been to Aklavik seven times. He is an ex-smoker.

The guest of poetry festivals all over the world, **Patrick Lane** has been called the best Canadian poet of his generation. In praising his selected poems, the *Vancouver Sun* described him as always walking "the thin ice where truth and terror meet with a kind of savage intuition." He is the author of twenty books of poetry, most recently *The Bare Plum of Winter Rain*, one collection of short stories and one children's book, and is, with Lorna Crozier, the editor of *Breathing Fire*.

Evelyn Lau was born in Vancouver in 1971. She is the author of *Runaway: Diary of a Street Kid* as well as two short-story collections, three volumes of poetry and a novel. Her most recent book is *Inside Out: Reflections on a Life So Far* (Double-day Canada).

John Newlove was born in Regina in 1938 and raised in a number of small Saskatchewan towns. He now lives in Ottawa, for his sins. His books still in print are *Moving in Alone* (the second edition, from Oolichan), *The Green Plain* (Oolichan), *The Night the Dog Smiled* (ECW) and a selected poems, *Apology for Absence* (Porcupine's Quill).

Stephen Reid's *Jackrabbit Parole* (reprinted by McArthur & Co., 1999) is the autobiographical story of a bank robber who escaped once too often. A biography, *The Stopwatch Gang* by Greg Weston, was published by Macmillan in 1992. Stephen Reid is currently at work on a stage play, *Heroin Elvis*.

David Adams Richards was born in Newcastle, New Brunswick, and for the last four years has lived in Toronto with his family. His most recent award was the Giller Prize for his novel *Mercy among the Children*.

Lois Simmie is an incorrigible genre-hopper, having written long and short adult fiction and radio drama; children's picture books, poetry collections and plays; and a historical true-crime book, *The Secret Lives of Sgt. John Wilson*, which won the Crime Writers of Canada Arthur Ellis nonfiction prize. She lives and works in Saskatoon.

"The Mama of Dada," **Sheri-D Wilson** has published four collections of poetry: *Bulls Whip & Lambs Wool* (Petarade Press), *Swerve* (Arsenal Pulp Press), *Girl's Guide to Giving Head* (Arsenal Pulp Press) and *The Sweet Taste of Lightning* (Arsenal Pulp Press). Her recently released CD *Sweet Taste of Lightning* (Swerve Sound) is accompanied by two videos produced for BRAVO! TV.

Marnie Woodrow, thirty-two, is the author of two short-fiction collections. Her poems, stories and essays have appeared in the *National Post, THIS* and *Write Magazine,* among others. Her first novel will be published by Knopf Canada in spring 2002, and her desk is currently in Toronto.